THE RICHMOND SLAVE TRADE
The Economic Backbone of the Old Dominion

Jack Trammell
Foreword by Alphine W. Jefferson

Published by The History Press
Charleston, SC 29403
www.historypress.net

Copyright © 2012 by Jack Trammell
All rights reserved

First published 2012

ISBN 978-1-5402-0636-7

Library of Congress Cataloging-in-Publication Data
Trammell, Jack.
The Richmond slave trade : the economic backbone of the Old Dominion / Jack
Trammell.
p. cm.
Includes bibliographical references.
ISBN 978-1-60949-413-1
1. Slavery--Virginia--Richmond--History--19th century. 2. Slave trade--Virginia--Richmond--History--19th century. 3. Slave traders--Virginia--Richmond--History--19th century. I. Title.
E445.V8T73 2012
306.3'6209755451--dc23
2012000248

Notice: The information in this book is true and complete to the best of our knowledge. It is offered without guarantee on the part of the author or The History Press. The author and The History Press disclaim all liability in connection with the use of this book.

All rights reserved. No part of this book may be reproduced or transmitted in any form whatsoever without prior written permission from the publisher except in the case of brief quotations embodied in critical articles and reviews.

Contents

Foreword, by Alphine W. Jefferson	5
Preface	13
Acknowledgements	17
1. Slavery and Virginia	19
2. Growth and Slave Economy of Richmond	42
3. Perspectives of Observers	69
4. The Economics of Slavery	80
5. Wall Street Goes to War	97
6. Broken Economy, Broken Human Beings	109
7. Legacy of Wall Street	115
Conclusion. The Opening of the National Slavery Museum	121
References	123
About the Author	128

Foreword

This is a valuable book because it analyzes the slave trade in Richmond, Virginia, as a case study using a unique framework. Moving beyond the usual macroscopic emphasis of simply examining the antebellum South as a static entity of masters and slaves, this work provides a paradigmatic shift in its analysis of the vast commercial and ethical contradictions, external constraints, internal dynamics, profitable economics, religious debates and traditional interpretations of antebellum America. Moreover, this monograph explores, on a microscopic level, the reality of the business of the buying and selling of human beings as chattel property. Hence, its emphasis on Richmond's becoming the "Wall Street of the Confederacy" accurately locates a set of physical places and spaces whose commercial, financial, monetary and psychological value is comparable to the value of contemporary Wall Street in New York City. In its totality, this book uncovers a missing page in American history in general and black American history in particular.

In locating the commercial aspects of the slave trade in defined physical places, this book imbues the intellectual discussion of "the peculiar institution" with archaeological, economic, historical, political and sociological meaning that extends beyond both its operations and its profitability. Consequently, the author had to literally look under bridges, expressways, rivers, roads and modern buildings in order to unearth some of the research contained in this monograph. Following chronological and linear timelines, the book examines how the development in the acquisition, delivery, movement and sale of Africans became a major part of both the South's and the nation's agricultural, financial, industrial, legal and political complex. Hence, the skillful use of multiple kinds of data—from plantation records to official government statistics, as well as other primary and secondary sources—confirms the book's thesis that during the antebellum period, the slave trade in Richmond was an essential and primary ingredient in the creation of individual, institutional, private and public wealth locally, regionally and nationally.

The ethical issues and religious debates about the justification of the trade in human beings created multiple divisions in many sectors of society. Although not examined fully in this text, these topics form part of a larger dialogue that placed the accumulation of profits before religious conversion and the maintenance of a stable enslaved labor supply above moral considerations. Indeed, it was the necessity for non-paid labor that became the most important element in the Atlantic slave trade. While blacks and whites were both indentured servants, notions of servitude were fluid. However, when various localities started to sentence blacks to terms of "service for life," various Protestant congregations argued over the righteousness of enslaving Christians versus non-Christians and whites versus non-whites.

Interestingly enough, the issue of color became so fixed and rigid in North America that many states passed laws defining "black" as anyone having any Negro blood. Thus, the daughters and sons of African women and European men were confined to the slave dungeons in an easy and convenient way to dispose of "the mulatto problem." The topic of mixed-race individuals shamed many white women and brought vehement denial from many white men. Consequently, in a total corruption of English common law, the question of a child's legal racial identity was settled when laws were passed that stipulated that a

FOREWORD

child's free or slave status was determined by the status of its mother. Therefore, children born to enslaved women were black and hence slaves, and those born to white women were white and therefore free. However, these stipulations in color and identity took on very complex meanings in Dutch-, French-, Portuguese- and Spanish-speaking parts of the African Diaspora. North Americans insisted on this bilateral racial dichotomy to ensure the purity of the white race and to prevent mongrelization and Negroization. Despite these rigid laws and practices, color consciousness emerged within both the black and white communities. Primary source evidence suggests that mulatto women commanded higher prices in some areas because of their desirability as domestic and household workers. Others were employed in brothels from Baltimore to New Orleans. Even though not frequently discussed in polite society, differences among those who were being sold and traded created a multi-tiered market structure. "Gentleman of Property and Standing" and other members of elite white society knew of, participated in and supported these exchanges indirectly. However, these kinds of commercial and personnel exchanges were not mentioned in patrician family circles. Hence, the slave trade created a hierarchy in its transactions that allowed many elite men to maintain "les mains blanches" (white, or clean, hands) while reaping enormous financial benefits from slavery in both the private and public spheres.

 The favorable location of Richmond, Virginia, and the massive and quick expansion of the slave trade made its economic viability very lucrative in this area. Given certain external constraints and suitable internal dynamics, Europeans found Richmond a hospitable city because it was established on the well-worn trails of indigenous peoples who had used the area as meeting places and trading posts for centuries. Indeed, Richmond's location on fault lines and navigable rivers that lead both inland and out, from and into, both the Atlantic Ocean and the Chesapeake Bay gave the city a distinct advantage as it emerged as a major slave-trading vortex. In addition, a rather mild climate and enormous tracts of arable land suitable for multiple

Foreword

agricultural crops and animal husbandry created an ideal "city upon the hill." Ships from Antigua, the Caribbean, New York and other American and international ports all came to Richmond. As a major part of the triangular trade, Richmond became a center for a rigorous exchange in human cargo, salt, tobacco and many other products. These items, as highly profitable commodities, would make Richmond and many of its citizens quite wealthy. Yet the respectable men who moved to the town let their agents, factors and seconds handle their unseemly commercial exchanges in order to maintain their genteel images of themselves as members of the landed gentry. Although many of their assumed aristocratic ranks and titles were bartered, bought and stolen, they maintained the illusion of having come from European royalty. Therefore, they had to let men of the lower ranks handle their business affairs.

Hiring out slaves was one of the major areas that created a great deal of elite wealth that was handled by contracted agents. These men set up the contracts and conditions and handled much of the day-to-day business operations for the men of means who did not want to be seen to be involved in a less than genteel pursuit. Yet this practice was challenged directly by those real enslaved persons whose masters told them to go to the city and make about fifty dollars and bring it back in a year. This system allowed for the creation of a separate and distinct black slave economic and social world that was not under the direct control or management of whites. Both domestic and foreign visitors to Richmond remarked at the amount of autonomy and freedom that enslaved men exercised as independent contractors to various businesses in town that needed the skills as specialized workers in tobacco, on the docks and with animals. Indeed, it is here that the line between free blacks and enslaved blacks working in cities was blurred and sometimes became dangerous. Harsh restrictions were routinely and quickly enacted immediately after an actual or rumored uprising. For example, after Gabriel Prosser's Rebellion in 1800 and Nat Turner's Rebellion in 1830, both free blacks and enslaved blacks working in urban areas were beaten, forced to endure harsh penalties for minor offenses and placed in jail without cause, and some were even sold into slavery "down south" despite having papers. Hence, blacks, whether free or slave, had to be mindful of their relations with whites who might exercise any of several motivations to sell and trade them from the area away from their rightful owners, where they would have no recourse to any kind of justice. The emergence of the "patrols" (informal bands of white men in rural and urban areas looking for blacks to capture and sell) served as a means of formal and informal control on the black population. Although renounced publicly by respectable whites, they were encouraged and tolerated by the demands of a dynamic, fluid and lucrative economic system that placed profits above human rights.

During the antebellum period, being a businessman was not a proper profession for a gentleman. Thus, these artificial distinctions in hierarchy created a large class of prosperous middlemen who contributed to Richmond's identity as the "Wall Street of the Confederacy." Only New Orleans had a larger aggregate in volume of humans bartered, hired out, leased to work, rented for timed contracts, sold and traded. Moreover, Richmond was number one in slave breeding, price manipulation and futures speculations. This volume's discussion of the ways in which Richmond's slave-trading markets were involved in outright capitalization, price fixing and market regulation is both fascinating and unique. Few historians of the antebellum period have ever mentioned this topic. Here, there are in-depth analyses of the actions and motivations of the individuals, as well as the gross monetary rewards reaped from these transactions. The assertions about Richmond's place as a financial center are validated with interesting data and vital statistics. Ordinary people placed advertisements in newspapers and on posters, as well as signs on doors and walls. They all offered Africans for sale or recapture. Many were quite explicit about the virtues and vices of the slaves. Other signs stipulated price ranges, and different ones offered flexible exchange arrangements. These primary source documents offer valuable insight into the formal and informal dimensions of the slave trade as Richmond expanded and prospered. Consequently, life in the city was fluid and fixed, formal and informal, rational and situational. Although there were regulations and rules, commerce usually seeks its own way, and often those ways extend beyond the boundaries of legal and legitimate society and accepted notions of propriety. With a vibrant commercial, seafaring and transient population, Richmond operated at many levels (some honest and honorable, others dishonest and vulgar), just as any other port city. These realities tended to bring many different kinds of businesses and individuals to the city. Many made Richmond home and shared in its dynamic history. Despite their own individual inclinations and tastes, part of that history was a vicious and vigorous trade in human beings.

While awaiting sale, the slaves had to be housed and prepared to garner the highest price. The most famous of those places was Lumpkin's jail. Virginia's well-established slave mart located near Lumpkin's slave jail and around the Shockoe Slip and Shockoe Creek constituted a contiguous area that was called "the Wall Street of the Confederacy" because of its fast and furious economic trade in human property. Blacks suffered tremendous brutality, cruelty, humiliation and suffering in Lumpkin's slave jail. Robert Lumpkin was known as "Bully." Some say he was given that nickname because he was cruel. Others say he tended to bully both blacks and whites alike if he were so inclined. Moreover, as a physical site, Lumpkin's jail and the larger Richmond, Virginia slave market remains for many African Americans a major psychological scar and represents unresolved tangible evidence of gross human injustice. Ironically, today it is part of the Virginia Union University complex, a private black school in Richmond. Only the contradictions and inconsistencies in American history can explain this unique situation. After the war, Mary Lumpkin, a former slave and legal wife of Robert Lumpkin, gave part of her estate to create the educational institution that would become VUU. That a man who was notorious for operating one of the most horrific slave pens in America could love and legally wed Mary, a black slave, is emblematic of the fluid nature of both race relations

Foreword

and the absolute power of individual elite white men to operate with autonomy and without restraint. In some ways, the slave trade in Richmond completes a circle. One day, perhaps soon, the people of Richmond can embrace the city's past and break the circle.

Alphine W. Jefferson, PhD
Professor of History
Director, the Black Studies Program
Randolph-Macon College
Ashland, Virginia

Preface

Wall Street (now 15th Street) and the surrounding blocks in antebellum Richmond, Virginia, between present-day 14th and 18th Streets, were home to as many as sixty-nine or more slave dealers and auction houses where tens of millions of dollars changed hands before and during the Civil War, providing the fuel that drove the southern economy. This wealth was central to the economics of the prewar South and even drove the national U.S. economy; it was also of central importance to the fledgling Confederate States of America after secession. In fact, the gross capitalization of slavery—the sheer scale of its value and economic impact—not only influenced the national economy before the war but also continued to influence the national economy even *after* the war and the formal abolition of slavery. This influence is partially evidenced by GNP statistics, which show that the South's portion of the national GNP fell from 30 percent in 1860 to a mere 10 percent in 1870. This was due in large part to the abolition of slavery, which essentially wiped out millions of dollars of capitalized assets instantly and worked in tandem with the physical destruction of the South's industrial complex to wreck the southern economy.

Preface

The more important story of Wall Street, however, is the role it played in extending human misery and unintentionally instigating changes that altered the course of American and human history—all to support an inverted economic structure that benefited a very small percentage of wealthy southern whites and, arguably, capitalists in both regions. "What ever [*sic*] endangered this Union, save and except Slavery?" Abraham Lincoln asked with prophetic wisdom. "The question of Slavery is *the* question." Until the last days of the war, however, when Richmond was erupting in flames and Robert E. Lee was on the road to surrender at Appomattox, no one along Wall Street in Richmond was listening.

The story of the Wall Street of the Confederacy is not found prominently in many histories of the Civil War, perhaps because it does not involve martial accomplishments and sweeping national narratives, but it is a story that must be told. In some cases, it is a story that is still buried under interstate freeways, lost in buildings torn down and even revised quietly in history curriculums in public schools. The story of the Richmond slave trade is a reminder of why recovering and renewing the appreciation of the most human elements of history remains so vitally important to the core principles on which the republic was founded.

A great deal of work goes into any project the size of a book; in this case, many thanks are due to the citizens of Richmond and concerned human beings who have already been telling the story of Wall Street, including but not limited to the Defenders of Freedom, Justice, and Equality; the Richmond Slave Trail Commission; *Richmond Free Press*; *Style Magazine*; the Richmond Department of Parks and Recreation; the Elegba Folklore Society; the City of Richmond; the Virginia Department of Historic Resources; ACORN; and many, many individuals, both in personal and professional capacities. The bibliography attempts to capture where I have specifically drawn on their work; most primary sources are also cited directly in the text. Many museums and archivists have also contributed their time and support.

Preface

Any errors of omission are mine and are not due to any lack of appreciation for the collective work that has gone into preserving the story of the Wall Street of the Confederacy. My hope is that this small book will spur a continued active interest in preserving and recognizing the vital importance of that history.

Acknowledgements

Special thanks to
The staff at the University of Virginia Library, Special Collections
The library staff at the Museum of the Confederacy
Randolph-Macon College
The staff at the Library of Virginia
The Valentine Richmond History Center
The staff at the Sargeant Museum of Louisa County
The staff at the Black History Museum and Cultural Center of Virginia
The Virginia Foundation for the Humanities and the Virginia Festival of the Book

CHAPTER 1
Slavery and Virginia

The story of the slave trade in Richmond is in many ways the story of Virginia. Slavery is arguably the darkest shadow to pass over the bright light of almost five hundred years of modern Virginia history. When the first Africans disembarked at the Jamestown settlement in 1619, near the confluence of the James and Chickahominy Rivers, it wasn't clear to any of the European colonists or even the Africans themselves exactly what their future status in the New World would be. There is some evidence that the twenty Africans—reportedly stolen from the Spanish and bartered by a Dutch pirate—arrived in the New World with a somewhat ambiguous status as indentured servants rather than in permanent bondage. According to Linwood Johnson and others, it is possible that they were not lifelong slaves, and the names of eleven of the first Africans are known, as is the fact that eleven of them were likely baptized as Christians.

Other black Africans apparently arrived in the early years as freemen. Some arrived in chains and died in the New World still in chains. The ambiguity of early black status in Virginia stemmed in part from the fact that Christianity and freedom seemed to be inseparable. Some of them also apparently received wages for their work, a situation inconsistent with outright bondage. This moral ambiguity was resolved in 1667 by the passage of a law that said that being a Christian would not necessarily alter the legal condition of slavery.

Regardless, by 1640, there were Africans on American soil reported as being slaves in the legal and fullest historical sense of the word. By 1640, their presence in what would become the United States of America was established historical fact. By the 1670s (and likely much earlier), there were African slaves housed and working at the site that would become the city of Richmond. By 1671, normal status as a slave upon arrival was established. There were at that time, according to Johnson, six thousand white indentured servants in Virginia and two thousand black slaves. The chattel system, with economics and a growing racism at its roots, spread rapidly westward from Jamestown to the new colonial capital of Virginia in Williamsburg, northward and then west into the wilderness settlements and plantations in what would become Henrico and Chesterfield Counties.

Eventually, nearly a full century later, the economic locus of slavery would become solidly centered on the small river village of Richmond, Virginia, situated on the fall line roughly fifty miles west of the Jamestown settlement. By 1860, nearly 250 years after the first African arrived at Jamestown, more than half a million African Americans had been bought and sold in Richmond's notorious slave markets and auction houses, part of nearly one million slaves eventually sold and moved south or west from the region. Eventually, the activity along Wall Street and the surrounding blocks in Richmond that were home to dozens of slave dealers and auction houses would become so economically successful as to obscure the roots of the original story.

The arrival of Africans in 1619 and subsequently in the Virginia Colony was fueled by a variety of direct, as well as more subtle, factors. Although slavery as an institution had existed in diverse forms since ancient times, a modern and extensive European model of it only evolved in the fifteenth and sixteenth centuries under the leadership

Slavery and Virginia

of the Portuguese and, later, with competition from the Spanish. The system was directly tied to the need for a large and easily controlled labor force to farm sugar plantations in the Atlantic and Caribbean islands and then, a short while later, on the New World mainland as well. The English were relative latecomers to the colonization of slavery, with Queen Elizabeth encouraging "heroes" like Sir John Hawkins, whose coat of arms "was an African in Chains," but they were always secondary in scale and importance in comparison to the efforts of the Portuguese and Spanish. Although the English were always playing catch-up with their colonial competitors at this stage of the game (1607), they would later help develop a slave system in Virginia and the American colonies that would make slavery notorious worldwide and a hot topic of controversy even in Western Europe, where it had its quiet beginnings commercially but was not overtly visible in daily life.

Slavery in Western Europe had never taken strong root as a social institution. This may, in part, have been due to some degree of social enlightenment, an attitude that permitted feudal systems and serfdom but also placed emphasis on political economy and some individual rights. In hindsight, it seems to have had equally as much to do with economics. Slavery simply wasn't profitable or economically desirable in Europe, and it was only the advent of mercantilism and the subsequent exploitation of cheap foreign resources and agricultural goods (and the comfortable ocean barriers that hid the worst abuses from potentially sensitive consciences) that made slavery abroad profitable and feasible. Commodities like sugar had high demand and large markets in Europe and could be produced cheaply on large, slave-driven plantations in the Caribbean, far away from polite circles in Europe.

The new English colony at Jamestown did not lend itself at all to sugar production. Nor did it have the abundance of gold and native wealth like that the Spanish had discovered in some locales more to the south. In fact, it seemed at first that the Virginia colony would have very little at all to offer, economically or otherwise, and instead was

The Richmond Slave Trade

Early engraving of the transatlantic slave trade. *From Library of Congress.*

hot, swampy, malarial-ridden and dangerous, with nothing tangible to offer in return for the risks.

Modern European-sponsored slavery was an economic entity, evidenced in part by the fact that African slaves did not go to the home countries in large numbers but, instead, went forcibly to where economic opportunity was the greatest and where there were no pre-established labor pools—in other words, to the colonies and to the New World. The concept of African slaves toiling in Irish potato fields seems so incongruous as to belie the real factors underlying an economics-based Western European slave trade and a subsequent North American system fully embraced by an independent American governmental policy. The American system of slavery began as a Western European colonial system but later transformed into a modern, industrialized, speculative slave system unique in world history.

Explorer John Smith of Pocahontas fame examined the terrain west of Jamestown along the James River, encountering the Chickahominy natives and other Algonquin tribes along the way, always looking for exploitable resources. He reached the rocks and falls where the future city of Richmond would be with Captain

Slavery and Virginia

Christopher Newport in May 1607. Above the Shockoe Valley and on rising land to the west (later called Richmond Hill), he encountered another in a series of small Indian villages. He likely had no way of envisioning that a great city and the economic and intellectual capital of North American slavery would reside in an urban center located there.

Although Virginia had little to offer economically at first, the advent of tobacco farming rapidly changed the economic equation. In 1617, the Virginia Colony made its first return export of tobacco to England. Less than three years later, nearly thirty tons of tobacco were received in the home country from the colony. Tobacco production was labor intensive, and as a result, a variety of labor arrangements were attempted, including forcing Native Americans to work (a failure, as they were vulnerable to European diseases) and bringing poor workers from England to the colony as indentured servants (many perished under the harsh conditions, and their availability fluctuated according to the European economy). In 1619, the first permanent Africans (from modern Angola) arrived, traded by a Dutch ship for food. The legal status of these first African Virginians, as already mentioned, remains vague—they were very likely indentured and possibly later freed—but it is also important to remember that the first ten years of the Jamestown experiment had been far from easy. In fact, it is safe to say that even as late as 1619, many colonists welcomed any form of human assistance that would help them overcome the initial survival struggles. It also appears that at this stage there were no black and white in the modernist sense of such identities—only free and not free. There are even recorded cases of Africans owning land and their own servants and, in fact, developing large plantations where blacks owned other blacks in enterprises completely analogous to white-owned plantations. This distinction of free or not free is evidenced by events that occurred throughout the new colony. African slaves captured from a Spanish ship in 1620, for example, were freed after their seven-year indenture fulfilled its course and went on to other free ventures.

The Richmond Slave Trade

Permanent slavery as a form of organized labor took hold slowly at first. In 1649, for example, there were still only 300 or so enslaved Africans in the Virginia Colony. This would change before long, however. Just a little more than one century later, Virginia would have roughly 300,000 enslaved Africans. Tobacco changed everything in the Virginia equation, and first families like the Byrds fueled their tobacco production with imported African slave labor.

By 1700, the majority of African slaves were engaged in tobacco farming or peripheral jobs. During the antebellum period, there were fifty-two businesses or factories in Richmond producing tobacco plugs alone. The rapid growth of the tobacco industry meant that producers could no longer count on inconsistent indentured white laborers, who usually worked a maximum of four to seven years on contract (limited legally), and the availability of whom fluctuated wildly depending on the economy in Europe and current social conditions. Tobacco production demanded a stable, large, long-term labor pool, and African slaves were seen as the easiest solution. Because black slaves were forced to stay in the labor pool for long periods of time, there was also time to train them as stemmers, dippers and pressers, thus creating a highly specialized, very inexpensive and very dependable workforce.

As the Virginia soil was slowly exhausted and production moved west, trains, canals and wagons brought the tobacco back east to Richmond, which became and long remained the tobacco capital of the world. They also transported slaves to Richmond to be bought, sold or traded, and the city became the slave capital of the New World.

Even later, after cotton became king during the antebellum period, many slaves were hired out not only as skilled laborers in the tobacco factories and warehouses but also as engineers, blacksmiths and artisans, so that regardless of their status and immediate job, the value of their hired labor increased exponentially, ultimately becoming like stocks and futures to be bought and sold on speculation. In fact, hiring out slave labor and speculating on future labor and slave property values

Slavery and Virginia

became more common in some locales than utilizing traditional field labor. Even during the colonial era, hiring transactions were common. By the eve of the Civil War, hiring transactions were five times more frequent than outright sales, according to historians Robert Fogel and Stanley Engerman. Hiring rates were typically at 10 to 20 percent of the slave's value, computed annually. An 1853 letter from Colonel T.J. Gregory to agents in Richmond serves as an interesting example:

> *Be pleased to write me on receipt of this what disposition you have made of my boy (James) that I left in your care last week. In the event of you hiring him out it will best I think to put him where he will be closely watched as he is a great runaway and in the event of your selling him will you not want power of attorney to make rights to him? You are aware thus my wish is to sell him as soon as I can something like a fair price for him say eight hundred dollars or upwards.*

Cotton may have historically fueled the Civil War (*Cotton Is King* was the famous antebellum book by David Christy), but before that, tobacco fueled a profitable Virginia slave-driven economy that underpinned everything behind the southern colonial way of life. Later, the practice of hiring out slaves meant that slavery could flourish even in a technical, highly industrialized, urbanized environment like Richmond or similar cities in the deeper South. Although not nearly as heavily industrialized as the North, the South, in fact, was transformed by the Industrial Revolution, and slavery adapted side by side with urbanization and industrialization.

Long before the Industrial Revolution, however, an equally important transformation took place in Virginia that was far more subtle. It's not perfectly clear in hindsight exactly when slavery became an entrenched legally protected entity, bound on one side by racism and on the other by an unapologetic profit motive. Although slavery was formally legalized in Virginia in 1660 (and Virginia was not the first colony to do so), important cultural shifts were clearly happening well before and after that date.

By the second half of the seventeenth century, something had changed besides the advent of the tobacco industry. It was not a shift that can easily be connected to a single event or to a single piece of legislation. Instead, it seemed to happen in incremental pieces, brought about by practical tensions and in response to events, and it occurred in different locations not always confined to Virginia.

One shift evident in the records is that Christian or non-Christian as a dominant identity dichotomy began to compete with white versus nonwhite as an organizing social principle. A 1640 Maryland case convicted a black runaway servant and sentenced him to servitude "for the time of his natural life," while his two white companions were sentenced to only three additional years of servitude. According to *Africans in America*, no white person has ever been sentenced to a lifetime of slavery, although there are numerous court records of whites having to sue for release from their extended indenture. By the time "Grace" was sold to Robert Garnett in Madison County, Virginia, in 1847, "slave for life" was the common marker in the bill of sale and was accepted as a "natural state of affairs."

In the rare antebellum cases where a slave served a term of labor before gaining freedom, he still remained at risk, as an 1837 anecdote illustrates: "Robey had got possession of a woman whose term of slavery was limited to six years. It was expected that she would be sold before the expiration period, and sent away to a distance, where assertion of her claim would subject her to ill-usage. Cases of this kind are very common." In Maryland, a free black woman was sold back into slavery, even though she had papers of manumit. Finally, in court, she was freed again, but stories of such occurrences became notorious.

These practices were not as clear-cut during the colonial era in Virginia. While it would be an oversimplification to say that the rules were made up by people in positions of power as events moved

Slavery and Virginia

along, it would be equally inaccurate to see the evolution of slavery and the slave trade in Virginia as a logical, linear progression.

In Virginia, the success of tobacco farming and the evaporation of indentured labor from European immigrants due to an improving home economy meant that African slavery filled a colonial labor vacuum. This was, as mentioned, formalized in 1660–61 when the colony officially recognized the legal status of slavery (Massachusetts having done so in 1641; slaves were also present throughout southern New York and some other areas of New England in that era; eventually, a large slave population was present in New York City and other northern cities). Within a short period, Virginia courts were further defining slavery by declaring that the children born of slaves were also slaves, by fiat, and later established the legality of killing slaves under certain circumstances.

It is difficult, historically or logically, to determine to what degree racism fueled the growth and acceptance of African slavery, or the practical need for cheap labor facilitated the acceptance of racism or both fed more or less equally off each other. There is evidence that the original settlers of Jamestown did not initially envision their fledgling entity evolving into a white-dominated and highly structured tobacco slavocracy. But there is also little evidence that they and their immediate successors took any serious steps to stop such a development from occurring. In fact, with no gold and no easily exploited natural wealth, the Virginia Colony was driven in large part by economic pressures at home in England that demanded *something* worthwhile come out of the Virginia experiment and, on the individual level, by settlers and adventurers who had an equal desire to succeed monetarily and socially. If either or both constituencies didn't make money and increase their social standing, then the experiment was a failure.

What is clear is that the end of the seventeenth century in Virginia represented a crossroads in the pathways of human history. While slavery was present in countless other places in addition to Virginia (more than 70 percent of all global slaves ended up on sugar plantations outside of continental North America), it was in Virginia where the powerful tension between a rough but predictable status quo and the governmentality of a new slavocracy that would redefine black and white relations in ways that would connect to everything from the modern civil rights movement to placing a man on the moon actually hung in a precarious balance. The men (and women) in power and positions of influence chose slavocracy, perhaps due primarily to economics, but nevertheless, they did choose.

"Southern conservative thinkers have long argued that slavery came to the South without decision," historian Mark Malvasi wrote. "As sinful but pious men, they were neither depraved enough to be utterly wicked nor brave enough to be entirely just." Yet they did make choices, both economic and political.

By 1700, those collective decisions were clearly making their influence felt in the area that would become Richmond. The city that would be worldwide headquarters for Philip Morris, the largest and most successful tobacco company, would also become the capital city of the slave trade and Wall Street of the Confederacy. By 1700, the area at the fall line on the James River was overlapped by westward-moving settlers. Plantations had spread into what would become Henrico County and all along the south bank of the James River below the fall line, then into what would become Powhatan County and increasingly to the west toward what would be the cities of Charlottesville and Lynchburg. Many of the plantations, as well as smaller farms, routinely employed indentured servants and lifelong bonded African slaves to perform the daily tasks associated with tobacco production, livestock management and other agricultural jobs and trade crafts.

The rising hills around Shockoe Creek—located on the north riverbank right at the fall line—were a natural focal point for local commerce to gather. In fact, the Native Americans had in the past periodically set up camp there to use the area just for that purpose. They had traded there with the newly arrived Europeans in 1607, when there were reportedly 150 native inhabitants living in a dozen

Slavery and Virginia

oblong branch-covered houses. One European scout stated that the location was intentionally designated by the natives as a place to annually leave the sick, the aged and the infirm to recuperate, where they would be dry and have easy access to fishing and hunting. If true, this would represent a unique kind of communal care in the native community that would not be seen in the white community until the middle half of the nineteenth century.

In the middle part of the seventeenth century, William Byrd I established a plantation known as Falls Plantation at the falls on the south side of the river. It lay approximately between present-day Hull Street and Stony Creek (then known as Goode's Creek), on the south side of the river. He established a trading post at Stony Creek that connected to docks that may have been the first to bring sizable numbers of African slaves into the area. Later, he built a warehouse on the north side of the river at the head of Shockoe Creek circa 1678, and there were certainly slaves working all through the area by that time.

In 1687, William Byrd II laid out the city design for Richmond, including the area near Shockoe Creek where soon the buying and selling of slave labor would flourish, especially since sailing ships and any type of river craft had to stop nearby due to the falls. Initially, trading of slaves took place right on the ships at anchor in the river. Between 1698 and 1775, at the height of the transatlantic trade, the ships arrived from Antigua, New York, Boston, St. Christopher, Barbados, London, Philadelphia and a variety of other waypoints. During these years, slaves left Virginia by ship for other destinations, including outside the colony.

Today's visitor to Richmond can walk a 1.3-mile-long trail between Manchester on the south side of the river, across to Shockoe Bottom and up through the area that would become the Wall Street district. The port of Manchester (originally called Rocky Ridge) became a major terminus for the transatlantic slave trade in the seventeenth and early eighteenth centuries, although trading also took place where the village of Richmond grew on the north side.

The African slave trade—slaves taken from a dhow captured by HMS *Undine*. *From Library of Congress.*

Slavery and Virginia

The Richmond Slave Trade

The unfortunate victims arrived in the holds of ships, often having to wait until night so as not to offend any polite citizens, and in the middle and late colonial era were increasingly marched north on this trail to slave jails and holding pens in Shockoe preparatory to auction and dispersal. Parts of the trail would become known as Wall Street (15th Street) when Richmond was more formally developed, a narrow street running north–south roughly halfway between 14th and 18th Streets. This would eventually become the commercial heart of the southern economy, the Wall Street of the Confederacy.

It did not take long for the slave trade to attract the attention of regulators, speculators and legislators. In 1698, neighboring North Carolina adopted a comprehensive and brutal slave law. In 1705, the Virginia legislature passed legislation declaring: "All servants imported and brought into this country…who are not Christians in their native country…shall be accounted slaves." This and countless other smaller court decisions accumulated like leaves falling every year until a system of regulation and complete enslavement was in place by 1800 that was elaborate, extensive, pervasive and legally entrenched. Between 1698 and 1774, according to historian Philip Schwarz, Virginians "bought" more than 100,000 slaves. Between 1700 and 1775, nearly 400,000 black slaves were imported into the American colonies.

In 1778, the importation into Virginia of African slaves was banned, a seemingly humane development. However, the domestic market had become so important to the economy that the cost of bringing slaves across the Atlantic far exceeded the needs on aging Virginia plantations for new labor. However, the movement of tobacco lands to the south and west, and the advent of cotton, would mean a sustained and booming market in the interstate slave trade, a business for which Virginia and particularly Richmond were perfectly positioned by geographic and economic factors. In 1800, cotton was 7 percent of U.S. exports; by 1860, it was nearly 60 percent. Virginia supplied the labor.

For some Virginians, slavery became beyond questioning as a second century of history evolved, fully accepted as a God-ordained

Slavery and Virginia

order to society. President Thomas Jefferson officially signed the end of America's participation in the international slave trade in 1808, yet at the same time, he was powerless to attack the domestic institution, which required for everything, he wrote sarcastically, "the consent of the masters." He spent much of his adult life troubled by the moral problems of slavery and the rigid defense some of his colleagues insisted on making of it.

Because most colonial slaves and many antebellum agricultural slaves were typically not paid any wages at all (excepting industrial slave workers in Richmond and a few others who will be discussed separately), and because their personal liberties were increasingly so restricted to begin with, the consequences for misbehavior and rules infractions were by definition limited to forms of physical punishment. What else could be done to a man who already had nothing and was not allowed to come and go as he wished? Virginia slave owners would hold by law the "power of life and death over the black men, women, and children shackled to their land." The infamous Richmond Black Code, like many others, mandated the issuance of the "stripes" for even minor offenses. It regulated such minor issues of personal freedom as where slaves could and couldn't smoke or when they could carry a walking stick. It also clarified who was black and who was not, essential to the categorization of race. By the antebellum era, black versus white had become the dominating dichotomy.

Slavery in Virginia was not a carbon copy of slavery as it evolved across the South, but it shared the most common brutalizing characteristics. As the value of slavery and slaves increased, the stake owners held in the health and longevity of their "property" naturally increased as well. There were even slave breeding networks that evolved, with owners and agents practicing physiognomy, an embryonic modernist version of social Darwinism that foreshadowed the massive human tragedies of the twentieth century. Many slave owners found great utility in ensuring the health and wellness of their investments. Nonetheless, the cruelties and excesses perpetrated on enslaved individuals cannot be mitigated by any other circumstances, no matter what the motives.

In Virginia, both a rural and an urban slave labor system arose, each with slightly different characteristics. Virginia also evolved a sizable free black population from 1800 onward that influenced in small but important ways the evolution of the race question. Some slaves, particularly in urban settings, enjoyed significant freedom to generate extra income and live independently. Others in rural areas were subject to hard labor without reward, physically abused and eventually sold south. The commonalities for African Americans (for by 1850 a higher percentage of blacks had parents born in America than whites, making them truly *American*) were a collective loss of dignity, restricted movement and opportunity and the shackles of racism and servitude.

By the antebellum era, hardly anyone denied that the system was based on the black and white dichotomy, with mixed races occupying a nebulous area that never quite fit into either extreme. This had not been the system in the first half of the seventeenth century; this was not Jamestown.

The laws governing slavery continually expanded in Virginia, extending to free blacks as well as whites who were slave owners. In 1793, for example, the general assembly passed a law making it illegal to bring free blacks into the state. In 1806, this law was followed up with a rule that gave newly freed slaves one year to leave the state or risk being automatically placed back into bondage for life. Eventually, slaves would be required to disperse within thirty minutes of church services and carry identifying papers at all times. Not even slave owners were immune to the legal tangles. An act in 1798 punished slave owners for allowing their slaves to sell any goods or merchandise, although enforcement of such laws would seem problematic by definition, and they were often counterproductive to agricultural slave owners who wanted to sell their products and naturally used their slaves to help do so.

Slavery spread to all areas of Virginia, including some where it did not enjoy the natural geographic advantages of the Tidewater and

Slavery and Virginia

Piedmont regions. In the Shenandoah Valley, where terrain favored smaller, family-style farms, German settlers were not naturally inclined toward owning slaves (and in their European roots, there was no history of such habits). Nonetheless, examination of the records indicates that they often succumbed to the economic and social pressures of antebellum culture and purchased slaves, both as an investment and to help with practical labor issues. A Lutheran congregation, for example, invested its money in slaves, even though it had little practical labor-related reason to do so. In fact, the pastor had the additional idea to rent slaves out or otherwise use the slaves to offset his salary and thus save the congregation more money to cover annual operating expenses.

In spite of examples like this, many frugal German settlers were anxious to disassociate themselves from the wildly speculative and unseemly nature of the Richmond slave markets, which seemed more than a little bit impolite and dirty. This is quite evident by the fact that many slave traders and speculators refused to use their personal names in association with the business names, both in Richmond and in other slave-trading locales. The wealthy and the elite tended to work only through agents or seconds.

People clearly differentiated between owning a family servant and speculating on the slave market. An ad for a slave woman in an 1818 Winchester newspaper made pains to emphasize, "She is wanted for a family in the Shenandoah, and *not* for the purpose of traffic and speculation." Kentucky passed a law forbidding individuals from bringing slaves into the state for speculative or resale purposes.

As might be expected, slaves who lived and worked on German farms learned to speak German, and this was unremarkable in the Shenandoah Valley. However, when a slave with such linguistic skills happened to end up on the blocks in Wall Street in Richmond, this might have caused a slight sensation. Sometimes, if English skills were in question, it might actually drive the price down.

As slavery spread, so did the slave trade. In small towns, auctions were sometimes held at designated auction businesses but more

The Richmond Slave Trade

Slave-trading block at Green Hill Plantation. *From Library of Congress.*

often at pavilions in the town square, in private homes, on the steps of courthouses, near public facilities like racetracks or at so-called "market houses." Most infamously, they were held in shady parlors, hotel lobbies or behind the façades of more respectable businesses. Some cities retain solemn but simple relics that reveal much, like Fredericksburg, where a notched sandstone slave block remains at the corner of Charles and Williams Streets—used to hold slaves in place while auctioneers sold them to the highest bidder. The stone is literally worn in places by the hundreds of arms that were bound in its grooves.

Public sales in the Shenandoah Valley, according to historian Klaus Wust, often "included slaves along with dwelling homes and farm implements just as in Tidewater, Virginia." Thus, there is ample evidence that slavery made its mark felt even in areas of Virginia that might otherwise have seemed naturally resistant. Complicating

Slavery and Virginia

matters, extended families in America were spread across both slaveholding and non-slaveholding regions, so that family members often inherited slaves, even though they lived in a non-slaveholding region or had no natural interest in owning slaves. They could choose to manumit the slaves but would forfeit considerable income in doing so. They usually chose to sell them, at good profit.

Another area where slavery did not root as strongly included the counties in the far western portion of the state that would eventually break away in 1863 to form the new state of West Virginia (see Table 1). Situated in largely mountainous terrain, slavery again had no natural geographic ally yet made its presence felt in some river valleys and isolated farming areas. Although antislavery sentiment would define the story of the breakaway of the region from eastern Virginia, African slaves were owned, bought and sold in nearly all the counties that would become West Virginia.

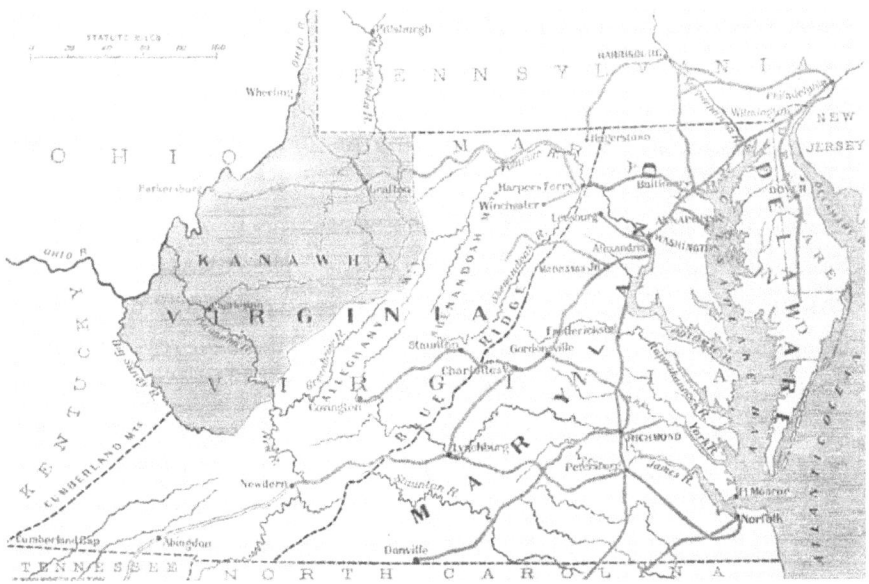

Proposed state of Kanawha in Leslies. *From author's collection.*

Table 1
Comparison of Western and Eastern Virginia Slave-Owning Patterns, 1860 Census

Region	Slaves	% of Population	Slaveholders	Per Owner
Western	18,451	4%	3,820	4.83
Eastern	490,308	30%	48,308	10.15
Total	508,759		52,128	9.76

(From West Virginia Archives and History)

Without question, slaves were a significant part of the economic landscape in western Virginia. In particular, more than half of the slaves in the late antebellum period in the Kanawha Valley were engaged in labor for the growing salt firms or were used in coal mines. Salt was the first major industry in the western portion of the state. Wheeling became a major western hub for the sale and hiring of slave labor, although never on a scale approaching the trade along Wall Street in Richmond. Many counties in the western part of Virginia held slave auctions at or near the county courthouse, or at the "block."

As events spiraled toward civil war, secret meetings were held in cities such as Wheeling and Wellsburg, where the call to action was: "Make western Virginia free, and she will invite immigrants. Her coal and her iron can be mined only by free labor. Negro slavery is wasteful everywhere, but less profitable [here]." By 1860, the western part of the state held fourteen so-called iron plantations where the popular desire was for free men to labor for their own wages.

As in Richmond, officials in the western part of the state created laws and regulations to attempt to regulate the slave trade, but as in Richmond, these efforts were undermined by the necessary freedoms given to slaves who worked in industry and had to move back and forth. Fueling the fire were incidents like one involving Reuben, a slave who was convicted in May 1861 in Lewisburg of

Slavery and Virginia

Slave auction in Richmond, circa 1830s. *From negroartist.com.*

conspiring "to rebel and make insurrection." A small arsenal was found in his cabin, and he was sentenced to hang. Had not Union troops occupied the area early in the war, there is no doubt that more drastic measures to control slaves would have been undertaken in western Virginia, just as they were in wartime Richmond.

In summary, slavery in Virginia grew into an elaborate system of chattel labor that included both agricultural and industrial elements, and it played such an important role in the overall economy that it functioned as a form of regional currency. Although not designed so in the beginning, by 1860, it featured legalized racism and protected inequalities that clearly were considered indefensible by many thoughtful observers inside and outside the region but were just as vociferously defended in arguments that always came back to a defense based on purely economic grounds.

Many tried to cloak slavery in biblical or historical terms or even argue that it was consistent with libertarianism. "Defense of slavery," George W. Bagby, editor of the *Southern Literary Messenger*, wrote, "was defense of republican institutions." Many Richmonders and central Virginians were hesitant about secession; some were abolitionists or opposed to the excesses of slavery. Their silence, however, was often taken as an endorsement of more radical policies.

The immensely powerful economics of the slave trade along Wall Street in Richmond meant that any real or imagined threat to the slave trade—or the larger slavocracy—provoked highly imbalanced overreactions that were rapid, ruthless and sometimes irrational, even by the standards of the time period. Until literal fire and overwhelming military conquest brought inevitable change and physical destruction to the slavocracy of Richmond in 1865, the system dominated Virginia, regional and sometimes even national politics and even dictated critical aspects of Confederate military policy during the Civil War.

No one knew in 1619 when the first Africans arrived that such a system would evolve—a system unique in world history in its complex economics and social governmentalities; a system that would take a major war and years of painful Reconstruction and civil rights initiatives to even partially dismantle. That it began in Virginia is a tragedy that did not culminate in Richmond with the 1865 destruction of Wall Street but still colors the politics of that city and that state even today.

Chapter 2

Growth and Slave Economy of Richmond

Great cities are often found along important transportation routes and at natural geographic features. Situated at the fall line along the James River, Richmond in the early colonial period was an innocuous village consisting of several homes, a blacksmith and one dirt street. Its location was driven by the geography of the fall line, which meant that oceangoing vessels could sail all the way upriver until they reached the rocks and falls at Richmond. Above that, the river became navigable again by flatboats and smaller vessels deep into the interior of the region. But due to the dramatic rock outcroppings and dangerous rapids, everything had to stop and restart at Richmond; thus was born a great commercial city.

The area had long been a Native American trading place, with frequent economic traffic and transient residents camping along the high northern banks above the river. Some original Native American trails are preserved today in part by the path of Park Avenue, which runs through the modern Fan District of Richmond. Westham Road also preserves a natural line noted by early settlers that was likely used by Native Americans.

Growth and Slave Economy of Richmond

John Smith is said to have been the first European to set eyes on "Richmond" when it was an Indian village (referred to as Powhatantown), on an early exploratory voyage shortly after Jamestown was settled. In 1609, Smith and his colleagues attempted to "buy" Richmond from the natives and establish a white settlement. The village was hence renamed "Nonsuch," as there was "no place so delightful," but the experiment ended in disaster and was abandoned shortly thereafter.

Colonel William Byrd II, who inherited his father's lands along the fall line at Falls Plantation in the Richmond area, was the first to begin to systematically develop the area. In 1733, he wrote famously of his grand plans:

> *When we got home, we laid the foundation of two large cities. One at Shacco's* [Shockoe], *to be called Richmond, and the other at the point of Appomattox River, to be named Petersburg. These major Mayo offered to lay out into lots without fee or reward. The truth of it is, these two places being the uppermost landing of James and Appomattox rivers, are naturally intended for marts, where the traffic of the outer inhabitants must center. Thus we did not build castles only, but also cities in the air.*

The village of Shockoes was located at the mouth of Shockoe Creek, a natural geographic focal point on the north bank of the river used by Native Americans for hundreds of years prior to European settlement. A port just east of Shockoe Creek called Rocketts was established with docks and small warehouses. Prior to the American Revolution, it was called one of the busiest ports in the colonies, along with the small sister port at Manchester on the south bank of the river. Around 1737, Major Mayo finished surveying the area on the north bank into lots. By 1742, there were approximately 250 inhabitants, and the town of Richmond was legally incorporated. The discovery and use of nearby coal fields both south of the river and in what would become western Henrico County north of the river sparked

The Richmond Slave Trade

Growth and Slave Economy of Richmond

economic activity. The Old Coal Pit Road was used to transport coal directly into Richmond proper.

African slaves were a large part of the growth of Richmond. According to the National Park Service, the *Virginia Gazette* dated June 16, 1774, announced a slightly larger than typical sale of slaves in Manchester: "To be sold 10th November at Rocky Ridge, 150 choice slaves, late the property of Jahn Wayles, dec'd by Francis Eppes and Henry Skipwith." Smaller transactions of a similar nature were regular occurrences.

Overall population growth was slow, however, and in 1768, the area was still relatively uninhabited. Of the more than four hundred original lots in Richmond surveyed by Mayo, only seventeen were "improved." Byrd's city in the air was neither a castle nor a city. Even shortly before the Revolutionary War, there were but two inspection stations serving only four tobacco warehouses. In spite of obvious geographic advantages and some growth north and south of the river, Richmond was not yet more than a tiny town.

This began to change during the Revolutionary period. As slave sales peaked at Manchester in 1775–76 and then tailed off, the population in Richmond passed seven hundred, and the city began to see slave trade on the north side of the river rapidly increase in volume. According to Schwarz, a number of special regulations regarding slaves were adopted in Richmond between 1776 and 1781 to deal with the traffic, including: strict curfews for slaves (though they do imply some daytime freedom); ordinances against meeting at night; and prohibitions on gaming, cockfights and horse races. Slaves were only allowed to sell goods on the weekends. Schwarz also notes that the growth of the trade in Richmond accelerated significantly between 1777 and 1782. In 1782, nearly half of the one thousand inhabitants of Richmond were slaves.

Opposite: William Byrd, early participant in the Virginia colonial slave trade. *From Library of Congress.*

The Richmond Slave Trade

The year 1782 also saw the founding of the first formalized city government, known as the Common Hall. City legend describes a gathering of common citizens along East Main Street on July 2 that included the election of twelve to serve in the hall. The first mayor was Dr. William Foushee.

Much of the early slave trading at the fall line had taken place aboard ships at anchor in the river, and even during the late colonial era, this practice continued. As the active slave-trading business that grew up in the town of Manchester on the south side of the James faded, the trade in Richmond proper began to compete with Alexandria, the other significant upper South gateway to the slave trade. When conducted off ship, the business was often advertised with red flags mounted above the doorways of taverns and small businesses, usually on court days (to settle accounts and debts), to signal sales. Even at this time, some African slaves had much more freedom than others, as reports from the area mention the constant coming and going of African slaves walking to the coal pits just south of Manchester.

During the Revolutionary War, when the trade moved north across the river to Rocketts Landing and Shockoe Bottom in what was by then Richmond proper, slave dealers and auction houses were among the earliest organized businesses listed in the city of Richmond registries. Within half a century, Richmond would be second only to the much bigger city of New Orleans in the amount of business conducted in human traffic and would overtake Alexandria as the gateway to the slave market in the upper South. Even much of the traffic credited to New Orleans often originated in Richmond. It is estimated that as many as 500,000 African Americans were eventually sold through Richmond before the Thirteenth Amendment abolished the trade, and in fact, the number may have been much larger.

Many attribute the phrase "sold down the river" directly to the slave business in Richmond, which eventually sold slaves almost exclusively "down" to areas in the Deep South and the near Southwest (Alabama,

Growth and Slave Economy of Richmond

Tennessee, etc.). The most frequent destination was New Orleans, literally at the end of the Mississippi River, but other common destinations were cities like Charleston, Savannah, Columbia and Wilmington. The common expression originating in Richmond ledger books was "Sold south!" or simply "South!" as is recorded on countless auction receipts.

The Revolutionary War finally provided conditions that helped Richmond grow from a sleepy river village into a more important economic center. In 1780, the Virginia state capital was officially moved from Williamsburg to Richmond, spurring additional economic growth. In the 1787 constitutional debates, delegates from the Deep South complained prophetically that a ban on the international slave trade would mean "slaves of Virginia would rise in value, and we should be obliged to go to your markets." Truer words could not have been spoken. In 1790, completion of the most

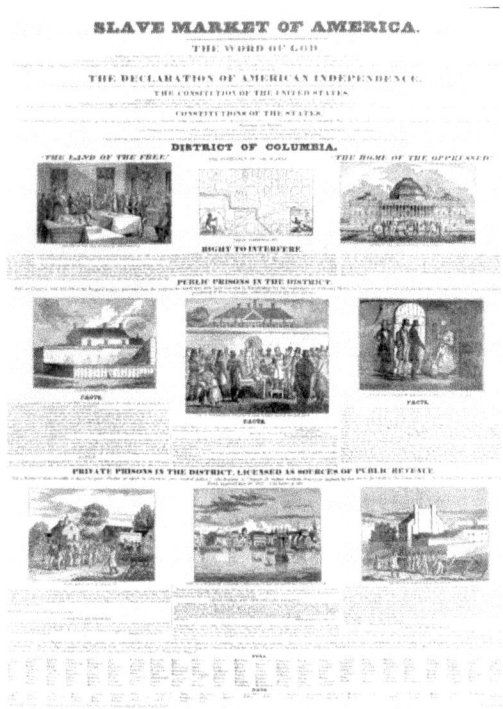

Gang of slaves journeying to be sold. *From Library of Congress.*

important section of the James River and Kanawha Canal increased economic traffic, as well. Soon, railroads would complete the slave transportation network.

Ironically, the U.S. ban on the importation of slaves that went into effect in 1808 actually increased business in Richmond, as markets south and west sought slaves from older, well-established slaveholding areas since they couldn't bring them in through the transatlantic trade any longer. This paved the way for the role of the agent and speculator, who bought low in Virginia and sold high farther south. By 1840, this also led to Richmond officials requiring slave traders to be licensed.

Although laws regulating the slave trade were fairly strict and record-keeping reasonably accurate by the 1850s, in the earlier decades such was not the case, and many transactions are now lost permanently to the sands of time. Like any multimillion-dollar business in almost any culture, there were also those who worked beyond the limits of the law and formal exchange and for which no written records exist. Because slaves were high-dollar commodities, the business attracted risk takers and those who would flaunt the law. One study by a historian found nearly ten thousand Africans "missing" in the 1860 Virginia census data—one possible explanation being that many slaves were sold "South" or left the state through unrecorded transactions (the historian terms this "emigration," although slaves did not have a choice of where to go when sold).

In the colonial period and even into the early antebellum period, slave transactions occurred not only in Richmond and on ships in the James but also on board smaller ships at moor along inland rivers, at private sales and in small towns. There were practical and economic reasons for this. Owners and buyers were obviously anxious to avoid the fees of the middle man, if they could do so in socially acceptable venues. State and local officials gradually came to the awareness that they had a tiger for which they couldn't grab the tail. On a practical level, it made it more difficult and sometimes impossible for authorities to tax or regulate the transactions.

Growth and Slave Economy of Richmond

Increasingly, however, the trade was drawn like a magnet to the natural benefits of geography, banking and transportation present in Richmond and took place near the city center along Wall Street (15th Street), between what are now 14th and 18th Streets. This area was convenient to the main commercial district, close to the river and the docks and later near several railroad stations.

The National Park Service recently recorded the historic area of Wall Street as

> *bounded on the west by 10th Street, on the south by the James River, and on the east by 19th Street. The northern boundary is more difficult to define because of the intrusion of Interstate 95 but it would approximate a line extended from the south side of Leigh Street on the west to the south side of Venable Street on the east. There are potential discontiguous resources near the Manchester docks and Rockets Landing. There may also be other related resources, as of yet not identified, within the boundaries of the City of Richmond and surrounding counties. The bulk of this geographical area is contained within three National Register Historic Districts—Shockoe Valley and Tobacco Row, Shockoe Slip, and Shockoe Valley and Tobacco Row Boundary Increase.*

The vast majority of the slave trade businesses between 1800 and 1860 were actually within a block or two of Wall Street, or 15th Street, which ran north–south down to the James River, a mere three blocks east of the Virginia capitol complex. Thus, an antebellum version of the more famous twentieth-century New York financial district dominated southern economic interests in Richmond.

Many of the buildings housing the trade were quite innocuous and served other diverse purposes. Again, from the NPS:

> *Within this industry there were a number of specialized structures such as jails, offices and auction houses. A number*

> *of public buildings, namely hotels and meeting halls, were also utilized as offices and auction sites. It has also been determined that a number of the slave dealers resided in the geographic area either in free standing buildings or on the premises of their business. For the most part these residences were not distinguished and part of the vernacular residential fabric of the city.*

Other Virginia towns and cities, even smaller villages, often supported a central slave auction location in the antebellum period that was as ubiquitous as a county courthouse or central park and bandstand. Photographs and sketches reveal that they were present in even tiny Virginia towns, as much a part of the landscape as other services like postmaster's or sheriff's offices. Very often, a wooden or stone "block" designed to hold the slave for examination prior to and during sale was a fixture; some blocks are still preserved in Virginia towns.

In Richmond, by contrast, the business of the slave trade commanded as many as sixty-nine establishments or offices clustered into an entire neighborhood—practically a small city within the city, a financial district. Some of the "jails" had elaborate fences, iron restraints and security measures. Some of the jails were literally referred to as "complexes."

The businesses that grew up along Wall Street—like those in Washington, D.C., New Orleans, Baltimore and other slave-trading centers—were often named in ways that revealed obvious insights into the nature of their business. They were often referred to as "pens," "jails," "dungeons," "gaols" or worse. The term "jail" was used even for agent-run holding houses like McDaniel's Negro Jail (and many letters are extant negotiating or complaining over the expenses of slave "jail" that owners were responsible for paying while their slaves awaited sale, hiring or repatriation).

One of the worst in Richmond—Lumpkin's slave jail—was also known as the Devil's Half Acre. Robert Lumpkin's jail complex, composed of various buildings, outbuildings, fences with spikes

Growth and Slave Economy of Richmond

Sketch of part of the Lumpkin slave jail complex, run by the notorious Robert Lumpkin. *From RichmondNeighborhoods.org.*

running along on top and connected yards, was the biggest in the antebellum South outside New Orleans. It was described in detail, as quoted in the book *Built by Blacks*:

> *Lumpkin's slave jail consisted of about half an acre of land near the center of the older portion of Richmond. The patch lay very low in a deep hollow or "bottom," as it might be called, through which a small stream of water ran very slowly. In approaching the place from the Franklin Street side, the descent was quite gradual and easy by means of a narrow, crooked, untidy lane. Around the outer borders of the said half-acre was a fence, in some places ten or twelve feet in height. Inside of the fence and very close to it was a tall old brick building, which Lumpkin had used for his dwelling house. Nearby*

> *were other buildings, also of brick, where he used to shelter the more peaceable of his slave-gangs that were brought to him from time to time to be sold. But in the corner of the plot was the chief object of interest—a low, rough, brick building known as the "slave jail." In this building Lumpkin was accustomed to imprison the disobedient and punish the refractory. The stout iron bars were still to be seen across one or more of the windows during my repeated visits to this place. In the rough floor, and about at the center of it, was the stout iron staple and whipping ring.*

In 2006, the James River Institute for Archaeology conducted investigations at Lumpkin's site and found, among other things, a cobblestone central courtyard, brick foundations and a very large retaining wall that divided the complex into upper and lower terraces. The excavation uncovered literally thousands of artifacts ranging from glass bottles to animal bones, and further digs may be undertaken.

Owner Robert Lumpkin would later illustrate the end of an era as he desperately sought to escape a burning Richmond in 1865 with the last of his chattel property. He led them in chains to the Richmond and Danville Railroad station, where Confederate authorities refused to allow him or his slaves to board one of the last trains out of Richmond. Lumpkin's jail would later be turned into a school for former slaves, the forerunner of the modern Virginia Union University.

Some of Richmond's more famous hotels also played a less glamorous role as convenient sites for slave trades. Agents and buyers would rent upper rooms and utilize "office space" on the first floor. Popular antebellum venues included the St. Charles Hotel located at the northeast corner of Wall Street and Main Street, which would later serve as a hospital during the Civil War (and where wartime advertisements for hired-out slaves to help with the wounded would run

Growth and Slave Economy of Richmond

SERVANT WOMAN FOR SALE.—We have for private sale a very valu able servant woman, a good cook, washer, &c. Apply to R. W. DYER & Co

In the same paper, July 20, 1846, Mr. Green advertises as follows :—

SALE OF HOUSEHOLD AND KITCHEN FURNITURE.—On Thursday, the 30th instant, at 10 o'clock, A.M., will be sold, at the auc tion rooms of the subscriber, a genteel lot of Furniture, worthy the attention of housekeepers, as the sale must positively take place.

Terms of sale: All sums of, and under, $20, cash; over $20, a credit of 6 and 90 days, for notes satisfactorily endorsed, bearing interest.

A. GREEN, Auctioneer.

UPON THE SAME DAY, AT 5 O'CLOCK, P. M., AND AT THE SAME PLACE, WILL B sold a very likely and valuable servant Boy, about 17 years of age, a slave fo life.

Terms of sale: One half cash, and the balance in 60 days, to be secured b note satisfactorily endorsed, bearing interest.

july 20—2taw1w&3taw1w   A. GREEN, Auctioneer.

For some reason the sale did not come off on the 30th, and accordingly th Intelligencer of July 31st, contains the following :—

SERVANT AT AUCTION.—The sale of the servant boy, advertised t take place at my store on Thursday, the 30th instant, is postponed until Thursday, the 6th of August, at 5 o'clock, P. M., when the sale will positively take place at my auction store.

july 31—cod   A. GREEN, Auctioneer.

Shame of the National Man-Trade.

In 1802, the Grand Jury of Alexandria said—"These dealers, in the person of our fellow-men, collect within this District, from various parts, numbers of these victims of slavery, and lodge them in some place of confinement until they have completed their numbers. They are then turned out into our streets and exposed to view *loaded with chains.*"

In 1816, Judge Morrell, charging the Grand Jury of Washington, said—"The frequency with which the streets of the city had been *crowded with manacled captives,* sometimes on the Sabbath, could not fail to shock the feelings of all humane persons."

June 22, 1827, the Alexandria Gazette said:—"Scarcely a week passes with out some of these wretched creatures being driven through our streets. After having been confined, and sometimes manacled in a loathsome prison, they are turned out in public view to take their departure for the South. The children and some of the women are generally crowded into a cart or wagon, while others follow on foot, not unfrequently *handcuffed and chained together.*"

In 1829, the Grand Jury of Washington said:—"The manner in which they (slaves) are brought and confined in these places, *and carried through our streets,* is necessarily such as to excite the most painful feelings."

In 1830, the Washington Spectator said:—"Let it be known to the citizens of America, that at the very time when the procession, which contained the President of the United States and his cabinet, was marching in triumph to the Capitol, another kind of procession was marching another way; and that con sisted of colored human beings, *handcuffed in pairs,* and driven along by what had the appearance of a man on horseback! A similar scene was repeated on Saturday last; a drove consisting of males and females, *chained in couples,* starting from Roby's tavern on foot for Alexandria, where, with others, they are to embark on board a slave-ship in waiting to convey them to the South."

Horrors of the National Man-Trade.

The Alexandria Gazette, as quoted above, adds :—"Here you may behold fathers and brothers leaving behind them the dearest objects of affection, and moving slowly along in the mute agony of despair—there the young mother sobbing over the infant whose innocent smiles seem but to increase her misery.

Left: An 1847 *Liberty Almanac* with slave trade news. *From Library of Congress.*

Below: Example of a slave bill of sale. *Photo by author.*

$1080   Richmond, Va. Feb'y 21   1861
Received of Joseph Silber Ten Hundred & Eighty   Dollars, being in full for the purchase of on Negro Slave named Henry the right and title of said Slave I warrant and defend against the claims of all persons whatsoever, and likewise warrant him sound and healthy. As witness my hand and seal

                    Edward Stager   [seal]
                    p. McKinney & Gurfrey

53

in the papers). Other hotels included the well-known Exchange Hotel on the southeast corner of Franklin and 14th and the Ballard Hotel on the northeast corner. They were eventually connected by a walkway over the street. Visitors with windows on the east side could look out over Shockoe and the Wall Street slave-trading district.

A typical ad from the Civil War era featuring the Exchange Hotel appeared in the *Richmond Dispatch*:

> *To remain in, or near the city, an able young negro man, about twenty-two years of age, also, a woman, good Cook and Washer, about forty-five years old, and a good Teamster (not restricted to the city) for sale or for hire the balance of the year. Apply at once to E.A. Cocke, Office on 14th st., Exchange Hotel Building.*

The Odd Fellows Hall, located at the northeast corner of Franklin Street and Mayo, was also a major auctioneering site. The firm of Pulliam & Betts did so much business there that it had permanent stationery and standardized sales forms printed for advertising the site. The auctions were held in the basement, according to Nina Mjagkij's *Organizing Black America*, and "announced by hanging a red flag on the basement door, these open sales of men, women and children led to an annual dispersion of over forty thousand blacks throughout the slave trading states in the antebellum years. During years of particularly brisk trade, this number could double as parents and children, husbands and wives and brothers and sisters were separated indefinitely." Later, Pulliam continued business there without Betts, simply crossing out Betts's name on the old stationery. Adding to the unseemly nature of the slave-trading business, many partnerships formed and dissolved within short periods of time involving the same general pool of traders.

Richmond's central role in southern slavery also put the city at special risk for the dangers of rebellion, violence and civil unrest. Richmond would be an important scene of two of the most

Growth and Slave Economy of Richmond

important antebellum slave uprisings (Gabriel's rebellion and Nat Turner's rebellion) and the political focus of several others. For every real slave uprising, there were dozens of rumors that remained unsubstantiated but influenced politics and public opinion. The constant danger of slave insurrection guided much of the state's domestic policy toward slaves in both the legal code and in the practical arrangements of the markets and trade houses. It also created ripples farther south in New Orleans, Charleston and other southern cities that connected to the Richmond market. Eventually, the laws in Richmond would become so restrictive as to defy logic. According to the website "Civil War Traveler":

> *Wary of this "at large" slave population and thousands of free blacks, city leaders restricted their freedom with the enforcement of laws that, among other things, barred all blacks from riding in carriages and carrying canes on the street. Blacks were forced to disperse within 30 minutes of church services and were made to carry their papers at all times. Those violating these laws were subject to penalties including whipping and, for the free blacks, being sold into slavery.*

In fact, there never was complete control. In spite of the sometimes Draconian measures, blacks in Richmond could not work and could not contribute to the economy without their hands being untied to a significant degree, both figuratively and literally. Therefore, a survey of the newspapers and personal letters of the antebellum period reveals an almost chimerical contradiction—slaves leased out by their owners, keeping portions of their own pay, living independently in neighborhoods in Richmond and raising families by choice yet still slaves and subject to all the potential evils consistent with it. Slaves began their own churches, though it was against the law to have a black minister, and the free black population of Richmond grew into the thousands, further blurring the lines as blacks worked, slave and freeman, side by side, mostly in solidarity to have community life.

There were frequent interruptions to this process. A major one occurred in 1800, when authorities in Richmond uncovered what appeared to be a vast, well-organized plot aimed at a general slave revolt. Gabriel Prosser was no ordinary revolutionary. Gabriel and his fellow slave colleagues were inspired and informed by both the American and French Revolutions and took an intellectual leap that none of the Founding Fathers ever could, drawing on classic Enlightenment thought about human nature and freedom. Gabriel's revolution might have exposed the hypocrisy of the Declaration of Independence and U.S. Constitution that talked of inalienable human rights had he not run into the harsh reality of the slavocracy.

Gabriel's rebellion died stillborn, as informants gave away the outline of it before he could take action. Unusual rainstorms also prevented a planned conjunction of his dispersed forces, which Prosser had prearranged to converge on the capitol. Nearly three dozen conspirators, including Prosser, were put to death shortly thereafter at the execution grounds north of Broad Street (near the current African Cemetery site), and authorities in Richmond, instead of acknowledging some of the moral difficulties with their system, instead looked to improve slavery regulations, establish a public guard in the city, strengthen the state militia and add further controls to every aspect of slave life.

The conspiracy demanded national attention, causing Virginia governor James Monroe to write to fellow Virginian and U.S. president Thomas Jefferson that the event was "unquestionably the most serious and formidable conspiracy we have ever known of the kind."

Gabriel had planned to burn Richmond—including the Wall Street district—down to the ground as part of his violent revolution. Although his sweeping plans died on the gallows, it would in fact take a conflagration of fire and military defeat to end the misery of Wall Street more than six decades later at the end of the Civil War.

Growth and Slave Economy of Richmond

First Baptist African Church in Richmond, part of a vibrant black culture in the city. *From library website, VCU.*

The second major interruption occurred in 1831, when a Southside Virginia slave named Nat Turner took up the violent cause of rebellion. On Sunday, August 21, while Virginia governor John Floyd relaxed in the capitol in Richmond and contemplated gradual emancipation and black colonization, the Southampton County slave known as the Prophet prepared his small band of renegades to initiate a reign of murder and mayhem later that night. Floyd's emancipation idea would run to rocks as a result of an inflexible state constitution and events surrounding Nat Turner's rebellion; the larger construct of black-white relations would also take a major step backward as a result of the axe-murdering, child-killing, alarm-ringing chaos that Turner initiated.

Within forty-eight hours, the entire state of white Virginia was in a panic, and Floyd found himself hamstrung by the same new state constitution in terms of what actions he could take. Basically ignoring the law that required him to consult with the Governor's Council, by midday Tuesday, Floyd had ordered state militia units notified by fast courier so they could converge on Richmond and other key cities and then Southampton County, as well. Turner's fantastic visions, revelations and ability to transfix his followers guaranteed that some slaves would come to his cause; the terrible, cruel and counterproductive violence of his movement just as quickly ensured he would enjoy little time or mercy from authorities. His efforts were doomed to fail but were again a dark prophecy of the destruction eventually destined for Wall Street.

The rebellion was put down, and the reprisals were vicious. New laws, ordinances and rules of hiring out blacks suddenly and dramatically turned in the opposite direction, back toward oppression, abuse and confinement. Whenever a problem arose, Richmond and Virginia state officials turned to the legal code to rectify matters. Within a decade, morals reverted to economic necessity, or the profit motive, and it was "business as usual."

In each case, the city of Richmond itself, housing the state government and home to the most sophisticated industrialized urban center in the South, as well as a vibrant news media, was without intention a central locus of a larger southern slave policy and an arbiter of wider public attitudes that in effect sent ripples through not only Virginia but also the entire nation. Ironically, the area around Wall Street in Richmond where the slave trade flourished was literally less than three blocks away from the capitol building, Washington's statue and many other important historical and cultural landmarks associated with Virginia's proud political heritage and leadership during the rebellion against Great Britain.

Growth and Slave Economy of Richmond

In the twenty years leading up to the Civil War, Richmond also provided an archetypal system of slavery and industrialization. In *Rearing Wolves to Our Own Destruction*, Midori Takagi shows convincing evidence that slavery in Richmond not only adapted to the Industrial Revolution but even flourished during it. In fact, the autonomy necessarily given out to slaves hired to work in the factories arguably sped up the eventual demise of the institution but, in the short run, served to fuel additional economic growth and impressive profits. Such slaves rented their own homes, paid for their own limited luxury goods and engaged in a level of self-determination that ultimately heightened the tensions between defenders of slavery and those who saw it only as an economic necessity or a blight to be tolerated on a temporary basis. Part of the defense of slavery had always been that freedmen (specifically, free blacks) could not handle the responsibilities of freedom. The hired-out blacks in Richmond's factories proved that dramatically incorrect (and there were approximately twenty-six thousand free blacks throughout the South proving it incorrect, as well).

By 1860, according to Takagi, "60.9 percent of all slave working men and women [in Richmond] between the age of ten and fifty worked outside of their owner's homes and received—to a varying degree—benefits including living apart, cash payments, and bonuses." In the Greater Richmond area alone, this applied to nearly five thousand African Americans. In essence, hiring out was creating conditions that fostered greater black freedom and proved that slavery was not preordained.

Between 1820 and 1860, many of the slave-trading entrepreneurs along Wall Street became busily engaged in leasing or hiring out slaves to businesses for a fee, rather than actually buying or selling them in a traditional sense. According to Fogel and Engerman, the normal time frame for hire was one year, although railroads, factories and other businesses sometimes "rented" slaves for the duration of a specific project. This proved extremely profitable to all parties involved. The slaves usually kept some wages for themselves, they generated income for their owners, they were less expensive to the factories than other skilled white workers and, of course, the speculators and agents made their percentages, too. Rates for "renting" steadily increased from 1800 to 1860, with the exception of the temporary economic downturn in the late 1830s and early 1840s. The normal rate of return on investment for renting a slave's labor was calculated at about 10 percent, much better than many other traditional investments.

A document from 1853 reveals the terms of a typical hiring out:

> *Terms of hiring the negroes belonging to the heirs of Wilson Mardre for the year 1853 are as follows. They are to have two summer coats, pantaloons and shirts, one good woolen winter suit-jacket lined through + through, the grown negroes to have two pair shoes + one pair stockings, hat and blanket—not to be carried out of county or employed on water except at the hirer's risk and to be returned to Yeokim Store on January 2nd, 1852, their taxes to be added to their hires + included in the notes.*

On this particular list, Toney was rented for forty dollars for the year to Dr. Warrock. There are nineteen other names on the list, with hiring-out prices ranging from twelve dollars up to slightly more than eighty dollars for the year. Yearly hiring rates would dramatically increase between 1840 and 1860. Another 1853 receipt from Captain William R. Richardson confirms renting a Negro for twenty dollars to Susan Exall in Richmond. According to some calculations, the average yearly rate of hiring out slaves in Richmond between 1800 and 1840 was roughly thirty-four dollars for females and seventy dollars for males; by 1860, it was much higher.

Terms between the owner and the renter were often negotiated by mail, much the way customers might barter at a Middle Eastern bazaar, only more slowly due to distance, as a series of 1854 letters highlights: "I would be willing to rent them out at the same prices,

Growth and Slave Economy of Richmond

Slaves waiting for sale in Richmond, 1861. *From painting by Eyre Crowe.*

but in the present situation she would be worth very little [since she was pregnant]." In an 1855 letter, E.L. Starling agreed to hire out two male slaves for $335 for the year, a fairly high amount, along with the caveat that they "return said negroes on the 1st of January 1856 *free of charge*." (Italics are mine.) All expenses related to the labor were fair game for negotiation.

The system of hiring out, as Takagi points out, arguably also sowed the seeds of the demise of slavery, however. A man who could keep part of his wages (as slaves in factories could and often other types of hire-outs could, as well) and spend them on what he wished was a man who was well on his way to obtaining greater degrees of freedom. Local and state authorities in Richmond recognized this but didn't have the economic willpower to do much about it, although from time to time they did tighten the laws that governed slave behavior outside of their work shifts. Within months, however, enforcement of such laws tended to slacken.

Reverend John Jasper (1812–1901) became emblematic of the confused and contradictory place that African Americans occupied in a slavery-driven Richmond. Jasper came to Richmond as a teenage bondsman from Fluvanna County and was subsequently hired out in various capacities. Due to the city environment and the slightly higher levels of freedom some hired slaves enjoyed there, Jasper was exposed to broader ideas and some freedoms. He was baptized into Richmond's First African Baptist Church and, as a result of his personality and perseverance, was eventually given authority to "marry slaves and minister to wounded Civil War soldiers." After the war, he was an early leader in the movement to equalize African Americans in the broader reunited culture.

Even with additional (but limited) freedoms, keeping some pay and often more than a taste of social autonomy, slaves who toiled in Richmond's factories remained slaves. Owners of slaves killed or maimed in industrial accidents often sought restitution for their financial loss; members of the slaves' family, if present, received nothing. Slaves remained personal property.

From the *Richmond Whig* on May 7, 1864, comes a fairly common notice:

> DREADFUL ACCIDENT. *Yesterday evening, about two o'clock, a negro man belonging to Mr. Jas. H. Grant, while at work in the Confederate arsenal, was accidentally caught in the gearing of some machinery in motion and received such terrible injuries that his life is despaired of. His right arm was wrenched off at the shoulder and thrown to a distance, and his right leg was so mangled as to require immediate attention.*

Growth and Slave Economy of Richmond

Such was the dehumanizing nature of slavery that the master is mentioned by name but the unfortunate slave laborer remains anonymous. Strangely enough, laws were passed protecting hired industrial slaves to avoid such accidents at the same time that laws were passed to restrict what little additional freedom they enjoyed.

The long-term effects of such laws of either type on business along Wall Street were negligible. The slave trade was too important and held the promise of an increased diversity of economic opportunities for investors, which led by default to increased sales. "America and its shame were inseparable," wrote one historian.

Those who suggested buying out the South from slavery were confronted with staggering costs. Mind-boggling figures were thrown about in conversations about possible economic emancipation, essentially torpedoing any possible chance at a real dialogue. In many ways, slaves became more of a currency than the dollar and served as an investment and a hedge against inflation and economic hard times. One can even argue that just as the United States later utilized a currency pegged to the gold standard, the antebellum South utilized a currency pegged to the chattel standard.

The effect on humans, however, remained an issue that stirred intense feelings across regions and cultural contexts. On his visit to the Wall Street area in 1853, the secretary of British writer William Makepeace Thackeray made pointed observations that were seemingly designed to stir up trouble. "I thought it might be possible to sketch some of the picturesque figures awaiting their turn [at auction]," Eyre Crowe wrote. "But, perceiving me so engaged, no one would bid...The incident was allowed to drop quietly, owing to the timely intervention of friends." In truth, Crowe felt threatened with physical danger for his "peek" into the inner workings of the Richmond slave trade on Wall Street. At one point, he was surrounded by a "whole group of buyers and dealers" who threatened him and decided the best plan was to leave. "Crowe has been very imprudent," Thackeray later wrote of the incident.

Ultimately, no one single person made much of an impact along Wall Street itself, although Crowe's sketches and later his paintings became associated with the wider abolitionist movement. In the grander scheme of politics, Crowe's art influenced the public perception about American slavery. In the narrower southern perspective on slavery, such critiques fell on deaf ears or resulted in scuffles or trouble, as Crowe found out at his peril. His inside look at the trade exposed to a broader audience how slaves were marched in coffles to market; poked, prodded and picked at to test for health; and ultimately sold like cattle.

At about the same time, a typical ad for a slave auction scheduled at Bell Tavern (where traders Dickson and Taliaferro had offices) appeared in the *Whig*, as business went along as usual:

> *By R.H. Dickinson: administrator's sale of twenty-seven valuable negroes. Will be sold on Saturday, the 2nd of January, 1841 at 1 o'clock in front of Bell Tavern, twenty-seven valuable negroes—consisting of box-makers, prizemen, twisters, stemers* [sic], *cooks, female house servants, and some first rate field hands. D.M. Branch Adm'r of Sam'l Cosby, dec'd. Sale conducted by R.H.D., Auctr.*

There were some ardent abolitionists even within the city limits of Richmond. Elizabeth Van Lew, for example, whose father was a prominent local leader, was an outspoken abolitionist and supporter of the Underground Railroad. The Van Lew mansion was a quiet stop in the escape network and a focal point of resistance to slavery. As a reward for her resistance (and many said spying for the Union), President Ulysses S. Grant made her postmistress after the war. Later, the beautiful Van Lew mansion on Grace Street was razed by the City of Richmond in 1911 for no obvious reason—some say as revenge for her volatile antebellum politics.

"She risked everything that is dear to man," a plaque in Shockoe Hill Cemetery reads, "friends, fortune, comfort, health, life itself,

Growth and Slave Economy of Richmond

all for the one absorbing desire of the heart—that slavery might be abolished."

Quakers have traditionally opposed slavery. The Quaker Meetinghouse in Richmond was founded in 1795 and no doubt harbored many who were openly opposed to all aspects of the slave trade in Richmond.

But the city registries for Richmond confirm that there were constant levels of vigorous economic activity present in the antebellum city slave trade that seemed immune to criticism. In 1852, for example, more than half of all the listed auctioneers and general commission merchants were also "traders," a euphemism for agents involved in the slave trade. In the 1852 registry, almost all the traders listed show their business location as being within two blocks of Wall Street, including such notorious dealers as the already mentioned Robert Lumpkin.

Resistance to the system was in most cases futile. A complex and sometimes even byzantine set of rules governed slavery, at times confusing even those who stood to benefit the most from it. There was also a curious mindset of resignation prevalent among many of those opposed to slavery that contributed to a damning maintenance of the status quo.

Slaves did resist or attempt escape. Apologists for slavery tried to explain slave escape attempts as "madness" or "ignorance," seeing blacks as child-like adults who were easily misled by abolitionists and northern radicals and who somehow were benefiting from the generosity of their owners without any real complaints to voice. Slaves attempting to run away were constantly being delivered to jails in Richmond, including Castle Godwin during the war.

The tenuous nature of the system, however, was also evidenced by a growing external criticism, a strong Underground Railroad movement in the late antebellum period and a print press reporting on excesses. Newspaper stories in the North were punctuated by eyewitness accounts from actual escaped slaves that sensationalized the cruel elements of the master-slave relationship. Henry "Box"

The Richmond Slave Trade

The resurrection of Box Brown in Philadelphia. *From Library of Congress.*

Brown, of nearby Louisa, Virginia, escaped from Richmond to Baltimore in a box after his family was sold south and then became a prominent spokesman for abolition. Brown had himself "shipped" via the Underground Railroad and then later went on to become a symbol against the tyranny of the status quo. A memorial along the historic Slave Trail in Richmond commemorates Brown's dramatic escape and later work (Box Brown Plaza, 15th and Dock).

Richmond slaves and others could try to buy their own freedom with monies earned from hiring out and industrial contracts. Even so, according to historians John Hope Franklin and Loren Schweninger, it was hard to avoid ending up in Richmond along Wall Street, even if emancipated. "In Virginia, the law required that emancipated slaves leave the state [immediately]…Since the neighboring state of North Carolina denied them permission to enter, and other states restricted their movement and ability to earn a living, those freed in Virginia faced the dilemma of leaving the South entirely [and immediately]." In fact, there are examples of emancipated slaves caught in Virginia after their one-year time limit expired and sold back into slavery, often

Growth and Slave Economy of Richmond

The Exchange Bank, through which hundreds of thousands of dollars of slave commerce moved, at the end of the Civil War. *From Library of Congress.*

being then sent South. As with all legal cases, there were instances of mistaken identity where legitimately free blacks were erroneously sold back into slavery.

Schweninger and Franklin also suggest that Richmond was one of the larger cities where escaped slaves, or manumits past their one-year grace period, often collected in attempts to merge into the free black community to hide and avoid detection. The city was large enough that they were sometimes successful in doing this, ironically, within a stone's throw of the massive slave-trading district, which bordered several black neighborhoods. But their life was in constant peril, and they were only one informant or "incident" in the street with the provost marshal or police away from returning to the blocks. A legal document from 1854 in Frederick County, Maryland, confirmed under affidavit that the woman in question was indeed manumitted and identified correctly, narrowly avoiding being sent back into bondage, but many more were erroneously (or knowingly) sent back into shackles.

Thus, through a variety of historical circumstances and over decades, Richmond became and remained a focal point in the slave trade that sustained a national economy and was responsible for untold human misery. The slave trade in Richmond set the trend for a vibrant and profitable interstate slave trade closely networked with other southern cities like Charleston, South Carolina, and also sustained the massive slave trade in New Orleans, Louisiana, that only ended with Federal occupation in 1862. Though housed in a dingy neighborhood and tinged with social stigma, the multimillion-dollar business along Wall Street touched everyone.

CHAPTER 3

Perspectives of Observers

It is not difficult, even by the vastly different historical and social perspectives of the given times, to find antebellum critiques of slavery and the slave trade both in the North and in the South. In fact, some of slavery's most vociferous opponents could be found in the Old Dominion itself, even before secession and the Civil War. There was also a small but committed core of defenders who, on paper, seemed to have no question about the morality or permissibility of the system. But most Virginians lived somewhere in between the extremes and were guided by a strange combination of personal morality and practical economics.

In what today seems to be blatant hypocrisy, many early nineteenth-century American commentators often referred to the Revolutionary War as a war against the tyranny of slavery and taxation without representation. Although they used the same English word to describe the domestic chattel labor system, they obviously didn't mean for the two examples to be interchangeable or synonymous. There were two kinds of slavery. One was typified by a governmentality of liberalism and a political economy that championed individual liberty over the chains of despotism and dictatorship; the other was a form of tacitly accepted racism that divided along lines of color and openly endorsed human bondage. Such distinctions were not clearly made in Jamestown in 1607. In 1861, such distinctions were taken mainly for granted.

It was largely accepted by many, both in the North and in the South, that Africans could not possibly gain from the benefits of liberty and democracy. "History affords no example of a people freed from slavery that were able to form a government that was free, or to exist in any manner as a free state; they naturally glide into anarchy or despotism," wrote one southern commentator in 1851. Yet many such commentators also suggested in the same breath that this was exactly what the Founding Fathers had done. The message was clear: African slaves could not understand or benefit from freedom; freedom and liberty were defined along color lines.

Sometimes, the hypocrisy was so blatant as to stretch the imagination of even a sympathetic critic, as when an antebellum southern doctor argued that the international slave trade was dominated solely by Europeans and New England shippers: "No *Virginian* engaged in the trade" (italics are mine). Virginians did, in fact, engage in the international slave trade, as Revolutionary- and colonial-era shipping records confirm. After the international ban, they engaged in a busy intracoastal and interstate trade until 1865.

Other examples of antebellum slave logic include significant southern support of the 1808 international ban on the slave trade because it would *increase the value of domestic slaves* or because it would *prevent slave rebellion* by keeping dangerous outside agitators from infiltrating the peaceful domestic system (italics are mine). The modern observer must attempt to check his or her own perfectly rational preconceptions in order to refrain from immediately assuming that these perspectives were ludicrous or illogical. At the time, they were positions argued seriously by reasonably intelligent people, many of whom were important people in positions of power and influence.

The slave trade in Richmond along Wall Street engendered a wide range of reactions from residents, politicians and foreign dignitaries

Perspectives of Observers

or visitors. It was positioned in the context that not all southern whites owned slaves or endorsed the slavocracy. Yet the institution of slavery affected all citizens, black and white, in very direct ways economically and culturally, as is evidenced by the many firsthand accounts that survive.

In written histories of the city of Richmond, it is made very clear that citizens of certain social or economic standing did not wish to be seen conducting business in the Wall Street district. Similar to the trading of slaves taking place aboard ships in the James River to hide from prying eyes, there was an element of dirtiness to it that defied apologists' attempts to justify the trade. Many wealthy southerners hired agents or assistants to conduct business along Wall Street for them or on their behalf. As a general rule, members of the state government, which met in the capitol several blocks away, did not conduct their slave business in person either but, rather, through seconds.

Perhaps in some cases they avoided Wall Street to avoid having to see some of the excesses that took place there. While "property owners" generally had good practical reasons to see their investments cared for in most basic ways—food, basic clothing, simple medical care—such a trade when tinged with racism inevitably led to incidents of excess. Robert Lumpkin, perhaps more notorious than most traders due to historical and more recently archaeological evidence available to researchers, was known for his rough treatment of slaves, including women and children. He was known as a "bully" trader in part because of his behavior (although "bully" traders also seems relevant to so-called bull markets). Ironically, Lumpkin married a black woman, Mary, a former slave. Mary would dispose of her husband's estate after the war and contribute part of the estate to what would become Virginia Union University.

The individual stories of the hundreds of thousands who came through Wall Street at one time or another add up to paint an inglorious picture. Slaves in Richmond, particularly industrial workers, were often damned if they did and damned if they didn't, forced to participate in a system that gave them certain advantages over other slaves (particularly traditional agricultural slaves) yet still kept them in bondage and subject to the whims of whites.

Moses Grandy was a slave who paid $1,850 for his own freedom and serves as a case in point. As he made the demanded payments, his master kept increasing the price. "I was hired out for the year, by auction, at the court house, every January," he recalled. "It often happens that, when a slave wishes to visit his wife on another plantation, his own master is busy or from home, and therefore he cannot get a pass. He ventures without it." Grandy's story captures the complex and irrational mixture of restrictions placed on slaves by a system that treated them partially as humans and predominantly as labor and property. In Richmond more so than in other southern cities (possibly excepting New Orleans), the mixture was complicated by industrial labor practices, a large free black population and significant white factions who were in muted opposition to slavery in general. Some antislavery factions met at the Powhatan House at 11th and Broad, which later became a breeding ground for the discontents who would form the breakaway section of western Virginia that would become the state of West Virginia.

Charles Ball was a slave sold south. He described the elaborate chain and lock systems utilized by auctioneers and masters to maintain control of their slaves. "[A]…sad reverse of fortune that had so suddenly overtaken me," he explained, as he was held for transfer, "[that] time did not reconcile me to my chains, but it made me familiar with them." Ball's account is remarkable for the lack of hatred or judgment in his voice as he explains the abuses heaped on him at every stop. The hooks, iron restraining straps, chains and other methods of imprisonment were part of the physical environment in courtyards, along walls and in rooms near Wall Street. Archaeology has uncovered some of the few remaining physical clues in the ground in the present time at the Robert Lumpkin jail site near Interstate 95.

Issac Williams was a slave sold to cover his master's debts in settling an estate. This was quite a common occurrence in the antebellum

Perspectives of Observers

South, particularly when a son had squandered a father's fortunes. The last-ditch effort to save the family from financial ruin would be to sell the slaves. "He whipped till he wore the lash off," Williams said, describing his angry master's financial frustrations, unfairly taken out on human victims. Auctions involving more than 100 slaves were not unknown when large estates were broken up; speculators, of course, saw it as an opportunity to buy cheap and sell high. One auction featured 346 separate slaves sold. In cases of inheritance, children were left to divide estates in court, as a case in 1860 North Carolina demonstrates, when great pains were made to be fair and divide the Negroes "evenly" among the inheritors.

One grandfather left a slave woman, Susan, to his granddaughter, making sure to indicate that the granddaughter also was entitled to all offspring the slave woman might have, called euphemistically "her future increases." As strange as it sounds to the modern ear, this was the equivalent of a college savings account set up by a loving grandparent.

Sometimes, it was a matter of pure expediency. "I have at last got the check," W.G. Hubard wrote with great relief in 1848. "I shall be in Richmond on the 30th or 31st of this month—shall bring up my servants to hire out and sell Moses. The fellow has conducted himself so much to my annoyance I have had to threaten him repeatedly that I find it necessary to end the matter in his transportation."

Hubard was desperate for cash, as he outlines in a series of letters. In one addressed to Captain Christopher Tompkins, Hubard complains of the difficulties with renting slaves out and especially the challenge of having his slaves properly cared for while in Richmond. "I was greatly surprised," Hubard wrote. "They [my slaves] complained to me so much about not getting anything to eat at the boarding house is the reason I took them away…I should have to stay in Richmond to see this matter entirely settled." Caring for slaves was a constant cost benefit analysis: care for them too well and it would cut into profit margins; care for them too little and, again, profit margins would suffer. Hubard, even though desperate for cash flow, was not willing to stand by and see his slaves mistreated by agents and crooked boardinghouses in Richmond.

Most Americans, by the eve of the Civil War, had developed polarized attitudes about slavery, largely due to the inflammatory effects of the print media and the ineffectual efforts of politicians to ease the sectional tensions. Those who visited Richmond and saw the Wall Street district firsthand seldom failed to be emotionally affected by it.

Charles Dickens was perhaps the most famous of many visitors to comment on what he saw visiting Richmond's slave-trading district. He found the city itself quite charming:

> *The next day, and the next, we rode and walked about the town, which is delightfully situated on eight hills, overhanging James River; a sparkling stream, studded here and there with bright islands, or brawling over broken rocks. Although it was yet but the middle of March, the weather in this southern temperature was extremely warm; the peach-trees and magnolias were in full bloom; and the trees were green.*

His descriptions of slavery and the slave trade were not so kind:

> *"Cash for negroes," "cash for negroes," "cash for negroes," is the heading of advertisements in great capitals down the long columns of the crowded journals. Woodcuts of a runaway negro with manacled hands, crouching beneath a bluff pursuer in top boots, who, having caught him, grasps him by the throat, agreeably diversify the pleasant text...all those owners, breeders, users, buyers and sellers of slaves, who will, until the bloody chapter has a bloody end, own, breed, use, buy, and sell them at all hazards: who doggedly deny the horrors of the system in the teeth*

Perspectives of Observers

Sketch by Eyre Crowe of the Charleston slave auction process. *From Library of Congress.*

of such a mass of evidence as never was brought to bear on any other subject, and to which the experience of every day contributes its immense amount; who would at this or any other moment, gladly involve America in a war, civil or foreign, provided that it had for its sole end and object the assertion of their right to perpetuate slavery, and to whip and work and torture slaves, unquestioned by any human authority, and unassailed by any human power; who, when they speak of Freedom, mean the Freedom to oppress their kind, and to be savage, merciless, and cruel; and of whom every man on his own ground, in republican America, is a more exacting, and a sterner, and a less responsible despot than the Caliph Haroun Alraschid in his angry robe of scarlet.

According to David Perdue, Dickens was extremely disappointed in his American experience:

> He was revolted by what he saw in Richmond, both by the condition of the slaves themselves and by the white's attitudes towards slavery. In American Notes, the book written after he returned to England describing his American visit, he wrote scathingly about the institution of slavery, citing newspaper accounts of runaway slaves horribly disfigured by their cruel masters.

Dickens wrote:

> [There] are those more moderate and rational owners of human cattle who have come into the possession of them as so many coins in their trading capital, but who admit the frightful nature of the Institution in the abstract, and perceive the dangers to society with which it is fraught: dangers which however distant they may be, or howsoever tardy in their coming on, are as certain to fall upon its guilty head, as is the Day of Judgment.

Thackeray's secretary, Eyre Crowe, later recounted how he and a New Yorker, who was on a tour of the South and happened to see the aftermath of auctions along Wall Street in Richmond, described the end of the process:

> After these sales we saw the usual exodus of negro slaves, marched under escort of their new owners across the town to the railway station, where they took places, and "went South." They held scanty bundles of clothing, their only possession. These were the scenes which in a very short number of years made one realise [sic] the sources of the fiercest of civil wars, and which had their climax when General Grant mustered his forces upon this spot.

Frederick Law Olmsted saw the city and wondered why the lower entrance to the capitol building had been walled up:

Perspectives of Observers

If the walling up of the legitimate entrance has caused the impression, in a stranger, that he is being led to a prison or fortress, instead of the place for transacting the public business of a free State by its chosen paid agents, it is not removed when, on approaching this side door, he sees before it an armed sentinel—a meek-looking man in a livery of many colors, embarrassed with a bright bayonetted firelock, which he hugs gently, as though the cold iron, this frosty day, chilled his arm. He belongs to the Public Guard of Virginia, I am told; a company of a hundred men (more or less), enlisted under an Act of the State, passed in 1801, after a rebellion of the colored people, who, under one "General Gabriel," attempted to take the town, in hopes to gain the means of securing their freedom. Having been betrayed by a traitor, as insurgent slaves almost always are, they were met, on their approach, by a large body of well-armed militia, hastily called out by the Governor. For this, being armed only with scythe-blades, they were unprepared, and immediately dispersed. "General Gabriel" and the other leaders, one after another, were captured, tried, and hanged, the militia in strong force guarding them to execution. Since then, a disciplined guard, bearing the warning motto, "Sic semper tyrannis!"

Later, Olmsted quoted another author visiting Wall Street:

Where the street was in which the brokers conducted their business, I did not know; but the discovery was easily made. Rambling down the main street in the city, I found that the subject of my search was a narrow and short thoroughfare, turning off to the left, and terminating in a similar cross thoroughfare. Both streets, lined with brick-houses, were dull and silent. There was not a person to whom I could put a question. Looking about, I observed the office of a commission-agent, and into it I stepped. Conceive the idea of a large shop with two windows, and a door between; no shelving or counters inside; the interior a spacious, dismal apartment, not well swept; the only furniture a desk at one of the windows, and a bench at one side of the shop, three feet high, with two steps to it from the floor. I say, conceive the idea of this dismal-looking place, with nobody in it but three negro children, who, as I entered, were playing at auctioneering each other. An intensely black little negro, of four or five years of age, was standing on the bench, or block, as it is called, with an equally black girl, about a year younger, by his side, whom he was pretending to sell by bids to another black child, who was rolling about the floor.

My appearance did not interrupt the merriment. The little auctioneer continued his mimic play, and appeared to enjoy the joke of selling the girl, who stood demurely by his side.

Thomas Wentworth Higginson, an outspoken abolitionist dismissed from his Massachusetts pulpit for his radical antislavery stance, had this to say about the slave trade along Wall Street in Richmond and possible local allies in his cause:

The biographies of slaves can hardly be individualized; they belong to the class…[but] the insurrection [Nat Turner's] made its mark; and the famous band of Virginia emancipationists, who all that winter made the House of Delegates ring with unavailing eloquence—till the rise of the slave-exportation to new cotton regions stopped their voices…Even the name of Turner was the master's property.

Perspectives of Observers

The voices of antebellum Richmonders about the slave market in their midst are sometimes hard to find. It is important to remember that just prior to the Nat Turner rebellion in 1831, the Virginia General Assembly had seen a very lively and not altogether improbable debate about the abolition of slavery in Virginia. But it is also noteworthy that outside the general assembly, there is little evidence of a wider public discourse that specifically concerned the Richmond slave trade.

Whatever local residents thought of the peculiar institution in general, they largely accepted activities along Wall Street as a matter of course. Their voices are largely muted in terms of historical sources.

Olmsted recalls a conversation on the train between strangers on the subject of a slave girl:

> *"What are you going to do with her?"*
> *"I'm taking her down to Richmond, to be sold."*
> *"Does she belong to you?"*
> *"No; she belongs to ——; he raised her."*
> *"Why does he sell her—has she done anything wrong?"*
> *"Done anything? No: she's no fault, I reckon."*
> *"Then, what does he want to sell for?"*
> *"Sell her for! Why shouldn't he sell her? He sells one or two every year; wants the money for 'em, I reckon."*

CHAPTER 4

The Economics of Slavery

The economics of human bondage on one level defies historical analysis. Econometricians Alfred Conrad and John Meyer acknowledged this when they said that economic arguments over causality have a "peculiar" impact on the interpretation of uniquely human events. It is ironic, indeed, that slavery is often referred to as that "peculiar institution," suggesting that it defies the normal types of scientific or phenomenological analyses that can be brought to bear on other social or economic phenomena.

Economic historians Robert Fogel and Stanley Engerman have been criticized for their 1974 book *Time on the Cross*, which was an econometric analysis of slavery that suggested that slavery was profitable, in spite of the negative impact it had on human beings and race relations. In some contexts, confirming the profitability of slavery also seems to have served as a surrogate endorsement of slavery itself, so deeply engrained in the American psyche is the profit motive and the need to keep it separate from moral issues. Fogel and Engerman's work confirms with alacrity and sophisticated analysis of census data what every trader and speculator knew without any books—that quick money and big money could be made along Wall Street.

The Economics of Slavery

Castle Thunder, in Richmond, where runaway slaves were temporarily imprisoned.
From Library of Congress.

In some traditional interpretations of slavery—including antebellum critiques by intellectuals both North and South—an implicit assumption was that slavery was an inefficient and ultimately an economically ineffective system. The so-called cliometrics of Fogel and Engerman shook the foundations of many myths about the slave system, and along with the works of John Ashworth, Conrad and Meyer, Eugene Genovese, Jenny Wahl and others that have by now lain to rest the notion that economics was not primal to the slave system, views gradually shifted.

In the present, it has gone mostly beyond question as far as most historians are concerned that the economics connected to slavery were not only a prime driving force behind its continued existence but also a factor shaping even its more purely human elements. To consider slaves—human beings—a commodity to be bought, sold, invested in, speculated over, manipulated, swapped, stolen or bargained for is essentially to dehumanize and categorize them into items like hogsheads of tobacco, bales of cotton, acres of land or ounces of gold. Yet it is precisely that process that made slavery such a powerful and change-resistant institution in the American South. Five American presidents owned slaves, as well as the majority of early Speakers of the House, highlighting the apparent hypocrisy of a nation that believed in freedom simultaneously with bondage.

The surviving records of antebellum plantations make it clear that slave owners treated their human property as both commodity and living persons, albeit as humans with inferior legal and moral status. To the twenty-first-century American mind, this dichotomy is troubling at a minimum, perhaps outrageous to many, but also illogical and incongruous, even by the given standards of the time. It is difficult to reconcile. To the eighteenth- and early nineteenth-century slave owner mind, it was perfectly normal and acceptable, but with contradictions built into the system that had to be ignored.

In "Visualizing the Richmond Slave Trade," scholars from the Digital Scholarship Lab at the University of Richmond describe the peculiar system in Virginia this way:

> *As central as the trade was to the state's economy, the trade itself was not openly celebrated in the state's political culture or literature as it was in other parts of the South. Most often, white Virginians did not mention enslaved people at all, and when they did, they were mentioned in ledgers.*

The Economics of Slavery

Virginians, and southerners in general, bought, sold and traded slaves the same way they manipulated other resources for profit and gain. But they also acknowledged a human element, even though it was often quite unintentional. Virginia slave owner John T. wrote to a friend in 1810 that he had a young slave boy he was grooming for a more specialized avocation and who therefore might be much more valuable in the long run than a typical field hand. He spoke of the boy's "potential" in both economic terms and human terms that seem quite contradictory today, yet this was a common attitude at the time among slave owners. In 1814, this same slave owner engaged in an argument, through mail, with a friend who was trying to arrange a slave swap that John T. deemed unfair and incorrectly priced the slave's potential value. This seeming contradiction— the treatment of a human in bondage as economic commodity *and* as a human being on some level—presents a problem to the would-be economic analyst of slavery. Very often, lists compiled to settle estates or for large sales note slaves beside other inanimate economic objects like corn or furniture, but just as clearly, slaves were not perceived as simply inanimate economic objects. Slaves were also transferred from one owner to another as part of larger financial agreements.

On lists of slaves bought and sold, subjects are often recorded by first name only. This is in large part because African slaves were not permitted personal surnames, only the name of their owner. On some lists, first names are supplemented with additional descriptors, such as Lewis "long hair" or Sally "with child." Although this practice was purely driven by practical concerns of identification, it also emphasizes the dehumanizing process of slave sales, trades and auctions. Instead of selling "Arthur," a receipt records the sale of "a negro man named Arthur." Although the semantics may seem minor, they were part of a deeply engrained process actually woven into a larger system of dehumanization. Primogeniture and even some aspects of western democracy itself have historically been predicated on the family surname, and African slaves were made less than human by its denial; they were intentionally "othered" as non-Western by their lack of surname.

Slave traders, as well as masters, were by and large reasonably concerned with the physical wellness of their "property." In fact, this was again an economic equation rather than an overarching altruism. The records are replete with directions to agents to arrange purchases of new clothes, personal articles, shoes, blankets and various items that would keep and present at auction slaves as healthy and fit and, therefore, more valuable at time of sale. A slave health certificate from 1837, signed by a Dr. Cabell, verified that the slave Erasmus was suffering from a hernia, a condition that would impact hiring and sale value for his owner, Philip C. Hausbrough.

Somewhat in conflict with popular cultural ideas about slavery, many states and locales had laws strictly forbidding the maiming or excessive physical punishment of slaves, not because it was morally wrong but because it would diminish their ability to work and their absolute economic value. Slave traders frequently made reference to a slave's scars being revealed and a subsequent diminishment of value. Slave owners often went to court to recoup losses due to slave abuse or mistreatment in the jails or to certify the legitimacy of disability, for which they then might demand restitution. It was particularly an emphasis in cities. When a slave's labor was leased out in the Richmond factories, he was hired in work on wartime fortifications or he worked in areas where his owner could not supervise him directly, the well-being of the slave was a constant worry for the slave owner; it was a matter of economic concern.

From the historian's perspective, treating slaves as purely economic figures is not practical or ethical. Consistent with such difficulties is factoring the degrees and nuances of human cruelty into the economic equation. There is no dollar value that can be assigned to freedom or dignity. Although the John T. already mentioned clearly displayed in his correspondence a level of responsibility for the health and welfare of his slaves and hired help—perhaps even

The Economics of Slavery

some level of affection for the young boy—he also placed orders for items he needed on his plantations, including "$1/2$ dozen handled whips, good quality, with thongs plain." The rest must be left to speculation (although in defense of John T., there is no evidence in this series of letters that he was usually cruel to his slaves and hired help). Either way, slavery's excesses and cruelties can't be justified or glossed over, no matter what the economics.

The total dollar value of slaves held in the South, expressed in historical dollars and controlling for inflation, generally represented a full third or more of all the liquid capital in the entire South. Expressed as a percentage, this was nearly a staggering 100 percent or more of the entire U.S. economic gross domestic product in certain periods, expressed as a comparison ratio (see Table 2).

Moreover, the North benefited economically from the slave economy in spite of all protests to the contrary. Most slave traders in Richmond, like Templeton and Goodwin, had multiple bank accounts in various northern cities where they constantly moved money around for commercial purposes (St. Mary's, Brunswick, New York City, etc., to name just a few for Templeton and Goodwin). Capitalism in the young United States of America found the perfect partnership among vast mineral and natural resources, growing commercial and urban markets and the science of industrialism—and cheap labor. Although the northern section of the country evolved much more quickly and profitably from an industrial standpoint, it did not do so in a vacuum. Northern and southern markets, sometimes divided by states that offered differing levels of local support and protection to specific industries, functioned as a type of nascent international-style capitalist market connected by steamship, railroads, common currency and a national postal system and fueled by inexpensive labor. The capitalist system encouraged the very processes that sustained an elaborate slave market and speculative culture, reinforcing the roles of property rights, capitalization and return on investment. Bridges, rolling mills, railroads—all were capitalized, speculated on, bought and sold and ultimately seen as mechanisms ending in production and profit.

The Richmond Slave Trade

Slaves were, economically speaking, the mills, rails and bridges of the South. The normal expected rate of return on slave investments, according to the Foundation for Teaching Economics, was roughly 10 percent. By the 1850s, future profits based on prices relative to rentals predicted that gains by the 1860s would be bigger than ever in the slave-trading business. This flies in the face of antebellum theories that slavery would die out of its own accord if left alone.

In very obvious ways, "King Cotton" was the consummate partnership between southern agriculture (fueled by cheap slave labor) and northern industrial processes and mill production (also benefiting from cheap labor costs). To see the regions as divorced is simply incorrect; the burgeoning industrialized and highly capitalized (including slaves) national economy was quite interleaved between regions and quite sophisticated in its drive for profits.

In a country where capitalization and expansion of markets dominated the thinking of the most powerful industrialists, it is no wonder that southerners argued so vociferously for a new Southwest region open to slavery; it is little wonder that they chafed beneath the notion of abolition, the economic equivalency of socializing an entire multimillion-dollar (perhaps even billion-dollar) private business sector.

What is more difficult to understand is how some historians have argued that slavery had little impact on the northern economy. On the contrary, when considering the gross capitalization of major industries and the amount of cash flow associated with large businesses, the slave trade of the South actually fueled economic growth in the North by creating a quasi-multinational economic movement that capitalized everything, including human beings (a modern example of this is the capitalization of pollution credits). On the eve of the Civil War, the slave trade arguably had more economic impact on the U.S. national economy than any other single type of industry.

The Economics of Slavery

TABLE 2
CAPITALIZATION OF SLAVERY AND GNP

Year	Slave Population	Gross Capitalization (in millions)	U.S. GDP Ratio
1800	893,000	446.5	93.8
1810	1,191,000	714.6	102.2
1820	1,538,000	1,076.6	153.1
1830	2,009,000	1,607.2	158.8
1840	2,487,000	1,740.9	111.7
1850	3,204,000	3,204.0	125.4
1860	3,953,000	7,115.4	163.8*

* Highest percentage in U.S. history prior to Civil War and Thirteenth Amendment
(Data from U.S. Census, K. Stampp and www.measuringvalue.org)

David von Drehle wrote recently in *Time* magazine: "The economic engine of slavery was immensely powerful. Slaves were the single largest financial asset in the United States of America, worth over $3.5 billion in 1860 dollars—more than the value of America's railroads, banks, factories or ships. Cotton was by far the largest U.S. export. It enriched Wall Street banks and fueled New England textile mills." Drehle also notes that this flies in the face of some historical traditions and perhaps is uncomfortably close to problems of economic disparity that still doggedly exist in contemporary America.

Virginia's chief antebellum export was not cotton, tobacco or corn but human labor—slaves—and the highly capitalized value of their labor. Of all the states in the Confederacy, Virginia was by far the leading exporter of slaves to other southern states by the antebellum era and encouraged the economy of slave trade through state legislation and local regulatory structures (Maryland also figured prominently but remained in the Union when crisis erupted). The sheer size of the trade and its impact was dramatically significant in terms of gross U.S. domestic product. In terms of capitalization, the slave trade centered in Richmond (and at the other end in New Orleans) was the largest single variable in the national economy. One slave auction business in Richmond did nearly $3 million in gross sales in 1861 dollars. Some months saw as many as ten thousand slaves bought, sold or hired in Richmond alone.

The modest firm of slave dealers Templeton and Goodwin serves as a case in point (see Table 3). Countless similar records show that large profits were at stake.

TABLE 3
TRANSACTIONS FOR 1850, FIRM OF TEMPLETON AND GOODWIN

Transaction Type	No. of Individuals	Gross Proceeds	2011 Dollars
Sold "South"	95*	$58,132	$2,325,280
Bought	31**	$19,005	$760,200
Swapped	4	$2,600	$104,000
TOTAL	130	$79,737	$3,189,480

*figure does not include children (7)
**figure does not include children (5)

This particular instance actually represents one of the smaller enterprises along Wall Street. Templeton and Goodwin did approximately $3.2 million worth of business in 2011 dollars. Another auction house, owned by Hector Davis, has records that reported more than $1.7 million in total sales in 1858, which would be more than $68 million in gross receipts by the 2011 value of the dollar. Even small operations, like that of Dickenson and Brother, completed gross receipts of approximately $20,000 per year, or approaching $1 million a year in 2011 dollars.

Like any industry that relied in large part on the capitalization of assets, slave owners had many options for insurance against loss. A

The Economics of Slavery

handbill, printed in Philadelphia but used in Richmond, serves as a case in point:

> *INSURE YOUR SLAVES! Thousands of dollars are saved yearly to slave owners, by Life Insurance. This renders them permanent property, equal to real estate!!! Insurance on Slaves for one or five years, the insurer having the privilege of discontinuing the policy at the end of any year; the Company obligating themselves to continue the insurance to the full term of five years, if desired by the insurer. Slaves insured between the ages of 8 and 60 years, to remain in Virginia, or to go and reside in any slaveholding State in the Union. All losses liberally adjusted. Losses paid in Richmond since September, 1854, $22,000. C.R. BRICKEN, M.D. General Agent and Medical Examiner. Office hours daily (except Sunday) from 9 to 1, and 4 to 6.*

Examination of a policy for "George" taken out by his owner, Joseph Myers, in 1858 in Richmond (Henrico County) for a five-year period, at a premium of $19.40, reveals some additional details. The policy was not valid if George passed "West of the Rocky Mountains" or if he was "employed as an engineer or fireman running a locomotive or steam engine." Nor did it cover any situation where George might die "by the hands of a mob." If in the unfortunate case of George's death Myer wished to receive the $1,000 payout, he would be required to provide a certificate of attending physician, certificate of acquaintance and certificate of the sexton or undertaker, which all had to be sworn or affirmed before a magistrate. In spite of the somewhat technical bureaucratic requirements attendant to such a policy, many slave owners saw it as well worth their time to insure their investments.

According to historian Mark Malvasi, quoting contemporaneous sources, many prognosticators both North and South believed that emancipation would bring economic ruin to the entire country.

A sudden and dramatic drain of such capital, instantly, would be something akin to a Black Monday. To downplay the role this economic activity played in the overall economic health of the country is no less than historic revisionism.

Slavery was immensely profitable. However, a large portion of that profitability was the result of the increasing speculative value of the slaves themselves. Nor did it involve small numbers of participants. Census data cited by the University of Virginia rebuffs the myth that only a small number of southern whites owned slaves (see Table 4). According to census data from 1860, 26 percent of all southern families owned slaves, many on a speculative basis as an investment or as a hedge against economic turbulence. Churches and other businesses also invested in slaves, even when they didn't need the actual labor. In Virginia, the percentage of slave-owning families was the regional average of 26 percent. The South in 1860 boasted sixty of the nation's most wealthy men, in spite of having less than one-third of the free population. Consistent with this, the per capita income on average in the South was $3,978, in comparison with $2,040 in the North. The slave trade was a direct influence on that material wealth; in fact, it was beyond comparison the greatest single source of that wealth.

TABLE 4

PERCENTAGE OF SLAVE-OWNING FAMILIES IN THE SOUTHERN UNITED STATES IN 1860

State	Percentage
Mississippi	49%
South Carolina	46%
Georgia	37%
Alabama	35%
Florida	34%
Louisiana	29%

The Economics of Slavery

Texas	28%
North Carolina	28%
Virginia	26%
Tennessee	25%
Kentucky	23%
Arkansas	20%
Missouri	13%
Maryland	12%
Delaware	3%
TOTAL	**26%**

(1860 U.S. Census, from the census archive site at UVA)

In antebellum Richmond, banks and other financial-related businesses proliferated at rates that followed the coming and going of slave-trading businesses. Although the banks were primarily located farther west in the city, the flow of money was steady and connected directly to the Wall Street district.

A historian of Civil War economics points out that in the United States in 1950—at the height of one of the most prosperous economic periods in American history—the rate of corporate stock ownership equivalent to the 1860 value of one slave among the general population was roughly 2 percent. This means that 1860 southern whites were more corporately invested in slavery (26 percent of families), by far, than 1950 Americans were corporately invested in a booming postwar American economy. On the typical southern plantation with twenty slaves, the slaves themselves (or their hired labor value) were worth more than the total value of the land and implements combined.

These figures further confirm that slaves were becoming more of a currency than dollars and cents. Hill Carter wrote to his cousin in 1842: "I think perhaps they [the slaves in question] would sell for $400 or $450 each, on twelve months credit, but I really do not think they would command more than $300 or $350 each cash, if that; I could not consent to sacrifice them without consulting." Although Carter wrote during a temporary economic downturn—one of the few periods between 1790 and 1860 when prices leveled or declined—it is equally as important to note how the slaves themselves had become like bonds or currency to be managed, loaned or hedged—even sold at interest on credit for long-term gain.

The ledger of businesses associated with the slave trade in Richmond just prior to and during the war is a sizable list (see Table 5). At least twenty-six of them were directly on Wall Street (Lumpkin's Alley at the northern end, 15th Street at the southern end). Although many conducted other forms of commerce in addition to slave trading (plantation and real estate sales, collection of debts, rentals, etc.), all on the list were engaged in the slave trade at one time or another (buying, selling, hiring, trading, etc.). As in the earlier colonial era, not all businesses were registered; an underground trade occurred beyond the licensure of the city that was an indeterminate amount of business. Many commission merchants didn't use their own names on transactions, a practice that contributed to the social stigma attached to the trade.

TABLE 5

PARTIAL LIST OF RICHMOND SLAVE TRADE–RELATED BUSINESSES, 1850–1865

Name	Location	Notes
Abrahams, W.	North Clay Street	
Alvis, Robert	West 18th Street	
Apperson, George W.	Birch Alley	
Atkinson, George Washington	Birch Alley	Large jail complex
Bagby, Thomas J.	Wall Street	
Ballard Hotel	NE 14th and Franklin Streets	Used by many traders

The Economics of Slavery

Name	Location	Notes
Betts & Omohundro	SW Broad and 17th Streets	
Blackburn, E.W.	Birch Alley	
Browning & Moore	Franklin and Wall Streets	
City Hotel	NE Main and 15th Streets	Used by many traders
Cocke, E.A.	Exchange Hotel	
Dabney & Cauthom	East 15th Street	
Davenport, Allen & Co.	Cary and 15th Streets	Part of building left
Davenport, J. & G.B.	15th and Cary Streets	
Davis & Deupree		Each also independent
Davis, Benjamin & Solomon	Wall Street	
Davis, Hector	Locust Alley	
Deupree, William	Mayo Street	
Dickinson, R.H. & Brother	NW Franklin and 15th Streets	Ad cited earlier in text
Dunlop, Moncure & Co.	Cary and 11th Streets	
Eacho, E.D.	14th Street	
Eagle Tavern	South Main	Used by many traders
Exchange Hotel	SE 14th and Franklin Streets	Used by many traders
Frazier, John	Broad and Mayo Streets	
Gouldin, William	13th and Governor Streets	
Hagan, Hugh	East 17th Street	

The Richmond Slave Trade

Name	Location	Notes
Hall, John	Locust Alley	
Hill, C.B. & N.B.	SW Franklin and 15th Streets	
Hill, Robert	Wall Street	
James & Williams	Virginia Street	
Johnston, Thomas M.	SE 14th and Main Streets	
Jones & Slater	Locust Alley	
Jones, George Harris	14th Street	
Keesee, T.W.	13th Street	
Kent, Paine & Co.	Shockoe Slip	
Levy, Ash	Locust Alley	Residence on 18th Street
Lumpkin, Robert	Birch Alley	
Lumpkin, Thomas	Birch Alley	
Martin, William	West 17th Street	
McDaniel, David	Birch Alley	
McKinney & Depuy		
Nott, Alexander & Co.	SW Main and 15th Streets	
Omenhiser, John	SE Main and 14th Streets	
Omohundro, Silas	SE 17th and Broad Streets	Exxon Station on site
Payne, John R.D.	East 11th Street	
Phillips, William S.	12th Street	
Price, Dabney	East 17th Street	
Pulliam & Davis	Wall Street	Each also independent

The Economics of Slavery

Name	Location	Notes
Pulliam, Albert C.		
Pulliam, Peter	Locust Alley	
Reese, Samuel	Birch Alley	
Slater, Leonard T.	East 17th Street	
Smith, A.	18th and Broad Streets	
St. Charles Hotel	Used by many traders	
Staples, W.T. & Co.	12th Street	
Sumner, George J.	East 15th Street	
Tabb, P.M. & Son	14th and Franklin Streets	
Tait, Bacon	SE Cary and 15th Streets	
Taylor, James M.	11th and Bank Streets	
Templeton and Goodwin		
Templeton, H.N.	Locust Alley	
Toler & Cook	Pearl Street	
Toler, John J.	End of 16th Street	
Tucker, Fleming	NW Clay and 18th Streets	
Turpin & Yarbrough		
Tyler, R.B.	Basin	
Walker, Edwin	NE Wall Street and Main	
Worthham	Governor Street	

(Data comes in part from a list in the City of Richmond's Parks and Recreation Department pamphlet *Seeing the Scars of Slavery*. Others are added by author as discovered in ledgers, newspapers and other primary sources.)

The Richmond Slave Trade

Map of the Richmond antebellum slave market in the Wall Street district. *Created by Elizabeth Kambourian.*

There were many other hotels and common spaces, like the Odd Fellows Hall, that also served as convenient sites for auctions and transactions.

When the Civil War broke out in 1861, there was simply too much money invested in the system for anything to change. In essence, this meant that the war would be financed by the capital of slavery; the war would be fought to defend slavery. It meant that business as usual would be conducted along Wall Street. In fact, the early part of the war generated a bull market like most traders had never before witnessed.

CHAPTER 5

Wall Street Goes to War

In antebellum Richmond, Virginia, the slave market was by any modern standard "big business." An experienced male field hand could bring as much as $1,500 to $2,000 at auction, or roughly $50,000 in 2011 dollars, and with the average rate of return on investment for a typical slave of 10 percent factored in and multiplied by a busy month's volume of ten thousand or more slaves sold, it is immediately evident that the Richmond-based slave trade of the early 1860s was a booming enterprise. Total gross proceeds in sales in the Richmond market alone would have equaled nearly $500 million in 2011 dollars in some years.

On the eve of the war, the district was described this way by the NPS:

> *The heart of the slave trading district was centered on these hotels and taverns and was roughly bounded by Broad Street to the north, Cary Street to the south, Fourteenth Street to the west and Seventeenth Street to the east. Locust Alley, which turned into Mayo Street north of Franklin, bisected the area between Fourteenth and Fifteenth Streets and connected*

The Richmond Slave Trade

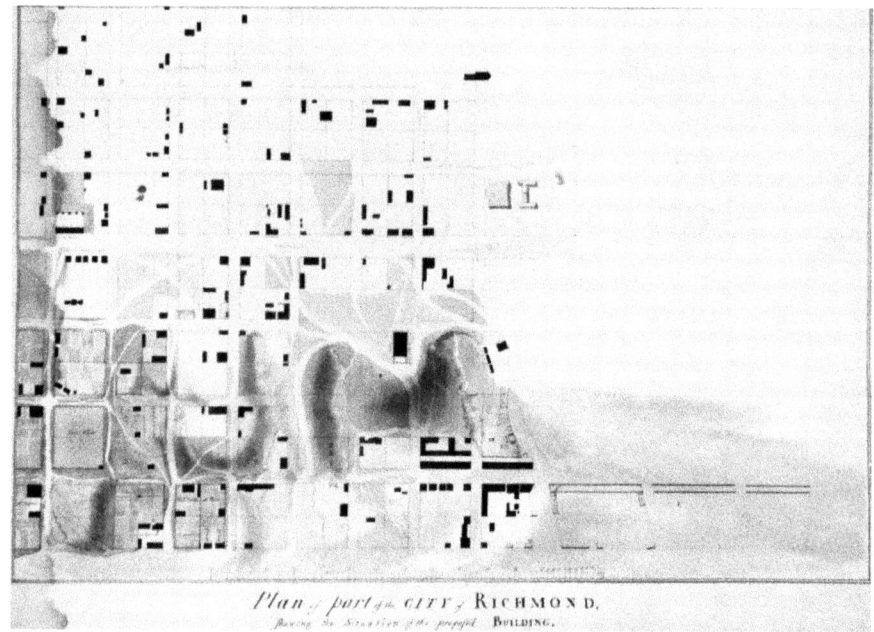

Drawing of colonial-era plans for developing the city of Richmond. *From Library of Congress.*

Broad and Main Street. Fifteenth Street cut an irregular track through the district, becoming Birch Alley, later Lumpkin's Alley, south of Broad Street, and Wall Street south of Franklin. Sixteenth Street terminated north of Broad and continued as Union Street for one block between Broad and Grace streets. Ross Street ran diagonally east to west just north of Grace Street and Exchange Alley bisected the blocks between Franklin and Main from Fourteenth to Seventeenth Streets. The irregularity of the streets can be attributed to the meandering path of Shockoe Creek that traversed the district. Several low-income residential enclaves developed in the Shockoe Creek area, close to the docks, factories and depots.

Wall Street Goes to War

Slave auction in Richmond in 1861. *From the* New York Herald.

This wealth, it has already been argued, was central to the economy of the prewar South, as well as to the fledgling Confederate States of America after secession and the formation of a slave-protecting central government. This enormous capital investment resulted in the South harboring 60 percent of America's wealthiest men in 1860 and a per capita income rate almost double that of the North. With nearly four million slaves at the beginning of the Civil War, the estimated property value or capitalized assets of southern slavery in 1860 was somewhere between $2 to $5 billion in 1860 dollars, or a staggering $150 to $200 billion in 2011 dollars.

The Richmond City Council found itself involved in the wartime slave trade as it replaced working white men who joined the army with hired slaves. Slaves were temporarily hired to work in the fire department, in hospitals, in the gas works and on fortifications for the city's defense. Other southern cities experienced similar trends.

THE RICHMOND SLAVE TRADE

Slaves were hired out during the Civil War to work in war-related industries in Richmond. *From Library of Congress.*

The city council minutes indicate concerns about the steadily rising costs of labor and complaints about maintaining social control in the city. "We see them [unoccupied slaves or free blacks] at every turn in the streets," one complainer wrote, "and see them lounging lazily in the shade, and yet the mayor and council are too respectful to their feelings to disturb them." In reality, the city council was forced to rely on hired slave labor far more than it normally would have and at the same time knew that it couldn't initiate routines that were so oppressive as to heighten unrest.

Wall Street Goes to War

The year 1860 was also the first one that Virginia law required slave traders to be licensed and registered. Had the war not intervened, eventually leading to the market's utter destruction, the system might have evolved even further into a sophisticated type of labor market unknown in the world's history, based on legalized racism and contractual employment. It might have changed the face of the modern labor movement (for much the worse).

This capital was critical to the war effort in countless ways, ranging from the work done by slaves in munitions factories to the work they completed on military fortifications. Midori Takagi reported that by 1862, "The largest single employer of city slave workers was the Confederate government." In theory, the negotiation for hiring such slaves for the government was directly with owners, forgoing the notorious agents and traders. In reality, someone was always after a commission or a piece of the action.

In Richmond, however, few gentlemen of high social standing would be caught even walking through the Wall Street area, a neighborhood of low-lying brick buildings and prison-like yards close to the James River, several blocks south and east of the capitol grounds. In contrast with the early days of the colony, when influential men such as Lord John Berkeley made fortunes in trading slaves, secondary agents, dealers or independent buyers now conducted almost all the business associated with the slave trade and were generally held in very low esteem by the population at large. Charles Lyell, a British visitor, saw one of these dealers who had made an enormous fortune in the slave trade but noted, "In spite of some influential connections, he was not able to make his way into the best society."

Nonetheless, the dealers and agents continued their work, generating, in Charles Dickens's words, "so many coins in their trading capital," after he witnessed the busy trade firsthand in Richmond. Slavery, too, remained the underpinning of King Cotton, the other billion-dollar industry that sustained an agrarian, elitist southern society and was the great international hope of aid for the Confederate government. As the

The Richmond Slave Trade

Slave sale in Richmond in 1861. *From the* New York Herald.

price of cotton fluctuated, the price of prime field hands also went up or down. The $191 million cotton crop of 1860 represented more than half the exports for the entire United States, and more than 60 percent of the slave population worked on its cultivation and harvest.

"The culture of cotton imparts to slavery its economical value," wrote David Christy famously in his 1855 book entitled *Cotton Is King*. Perhaps, following the argument made in this text, it was actually slavery that drove the value of cotton. In the city of Richmond, the value of slavery and its connections to King Cotton also helped foster an elaborate sub-economy of related support services: ships' captains and their crews, merchants, railroad personnel, police, tradesmen and, of course, bankers.

Agents also served as pricing advisors. When owners or estate administrators prepared to sell or hire out slaves, they often

Wall Street Goes to War

approached dealers, like Dickinson and Brother in Richmond, to find out exactly what their slave or slaves were worth. "Please gain me by the cost of boarding...and present prices of negroes," A. Dudley wrote to the firm in 1860. "Please advise of your opinion."

In fact, after the abolition of the international slave trade to the United States in 1808, other states and cities complained about the growing monopoly Richmond enjoyed in the interstate slave trade. By 1840, Richmond authorities began requiring slave traders to be licensed, a clear indication of the growing revenues. Not long afterward, taxes were levied on slave-pen owners. By 1860, it was state law in Virginia for slave traders to obtain a state license, as well as any local licenses. By the start of the Civil War, more than half a million slaves had moved through the Virginia slave markets to points farther south or west, and the first two years of the Civil War were some of the busiest ever along Wall Street.

"Dear brother," Henry Tayloe wrote, "The present high price of Negroes can not [sic] continue long and if you will make me a partner in the sale on reasonable terms I will bring them out this Fall from VA and sell them for you and release you from all troubles."

Civil War Richmond was ideally suited to the interstate slave trade due to the development of an effective transportation system that included five railroads, a major navigable river with access to the Chesapeake Bay and Atlantic Ocean (and a port, Rocketts Landing, which included extensive docks on both sides of the river), several canals and a series of major north–south and east–west roads. A slavery-friendly central government located—as fate would have it—in Richmond, too, also helped fuel an early wartime surge in the slave trade.

Originally, trading had taken place on-board ships at dock in the river, but by the Civil War, the business had moved almost completely to the Wall Street district. By 1820, Richmond had essentially cornered the interstate slave market, and ironically, this thriving business fueled continued Virginian support for the ban on the international slave trade (since domestic slaves sold for much higher prices than imported African slaves). At the beginning of the Civil War, the Confederate government began to print paper money and bonds, often with vignettes of slavery on them.

Slaves were essentially *the* currency in the antebellum South. "Slavery did provide the basis of status, wealth, and power," historian Mark Malvasi wrote. When playboy planter Pierce Butler exhausted his fortune gambling, he resorted to selling his entire stable of chattel to recover his debt. The sale, conducted at a racetrack in Savannah, Georgia, netted him more than $300,000 (approximately $12 million in 2011 dollars) and allowed him to temporarily prolong his lavish lifestyle. Likewise, slavery sustained a Confederate government that made economic decisions based on its assumed prosperity.

During bull markets at the beginning of the war, so-called traders (sometimes just unemployed opportunists who were not licensed) traveled around Virginia and other southern states buying up slaves to take to Richmond and sell at profit. At such times, the pens in Richmond were crowded with the chaotic traffic of human misery, and even some hardhearted proslavery advocates had to turn their eyes away. During the war years, patrols were often formed of local militia who would look for army deserters and runaway slaves. When caught, runaways often ended up in the gaols of Wall Street in Richmond. On occasions more common than owners wanted to admit, other businesses knowingly hired runaways at discount rates, which was cheaper than hiring them through agents in Richmond and, of course, eliminating the cut that went back to the owner.

There were laws, sometimes controversial, that dealt harshly with runaway slaves, as well as with those who aided or abetted them. "Any person harboring or employing said Negro will be dealt with to the utmost rigor of the law," many ads for runaway slaves read. Nonetheless, the chaos of war often presented opportunities for slaves to slip away. When they were caught, they were hauled off to the nearest slave jail.

Robert Lumpkin's slave jail, known as the "Devil's Half Acre" and already mentioned several times, was perhaps the most notorious

Wall Street Goes to War

of the dozens of businesses that supported the interstate traffic in Civil War Richmond. Situated on the east side of Lumpkin's Alley (which turned into Wall Street one block farther south), Lumpkin's consisted of a stockade fence surrounding six wooden buildings, two of which were large, two-story dormitories for men and women. The other buildings served as kitchen, laundry, supply shed and office. Since healthy slaves brought better prices, slaves were usually given fresh clothing and treated for any maladies suffered during transport. Under normal circumstances, Lumpkin's served more as a collection point for incoming slaves and not an actual point of sale. After being bathed and healed, the slaves were shuttled out to the various auction houses and dealers in the Shockoe Bottom area. Almost all the slaves sold in Richmond ended up farther south, and many of them went to large plantations in Louisiana or on to further resale in New Orleans or Charleston, South Carolina. During the war, thousands were hired out on behalf of the Confederate government. Lumpkin was perhaps the most notorious and the most typical of the era. His compound included his personal residence (where his wife, a former slave, lived with him), as well as a hotel-like area for guests and buyers to stay.

Enforcement of slave laws and keeping general order in the city fell to the provost marshal, Brigadier General John H. Winder, for much of the war, and his company was always vigorously avoided by blacks and whites alike. A trip to his headquarters at 10th and Broad Streets was not a pleasant prospect, particularly as the odor from the uniforms and clothing taken off dead soldiers had a tendency to drift upward from the basement, where thousands of them were stored. Winder was a man no citizen wished to meet anywhere, least of all at his office.

Security of "property" was a constant struggle. The *Richmond Whig* of June 30, 1862, ran the following notice, very typical of the time:

> *RANAWAY from the 2d Division of Winder Hospital on the 15th of the present month, two negro men, named Nat and Dudley. Nat was hired of N. Welsh, of the city of*

The Richmond Slave Trade

> *Richmond, is about 80 years of age, black, about 5 feet 8 or 9 inches high, with a scar under one eye. Dudley was hired of Mr. Allsop, of Pittsylvania county [sic], Va., is about 35 years of age, dark copper color, about 5 feet 10 or 11 inches high. A liberal reward will be paid for the apprehension of these negroes and their deliverance to me at Winder Hospital. The owners of said negroes are hereby notified of their absence. The Provost Guard is also requested to use their endeavors to apprehend them. A.G. Lane, Chief Surgeon Winder Hospital.*

Runaway slaves were, as always, subject to harsh reprisals, and during the war, countless of those recaptured were held in the jails around Wall Street, awaiting punishment and disposal. Sometimes, as in the case of Gabriel, the slave rebellion leader, they were executed and buried at the African Burial Ground, just north of 15th and Broad Streets, at the north end of the Wall Street district. Modern visitors can visit this site, now with signs and markers, which is also beside where Lumpkin's infamous slave dealership was located. More often than not, masters would be responsible for paying jail fees to house recaptured slaves until they were repatriated to their owners. Such was the case in an 1852 list of expenses for Nelson, for example, a slave who was returned to his owner after the bill for $108.20 was paid to the jailer. In other cases, owners instituted special terms of sale, as in this 1853 letter to Richmond agents: "I send...my negro woman Jamey...to sale. You will please do the best you can for me, with the distinct understanding that she is never to return to Caroline County again under any circumstances." There were many reasons this owner may not have wanted her to return.

As wartime inflation and confidence in the Confederate government waned, the older business sections of Richmond saw the proliferation of auction houses outside of Wall Street to expedite the transfer of personal property. Old families lost fortunes, while profiteers made fortunes. Gambling, prostitution and petty theft were rampant in the city, in spite of the efforts of Winder and city police. So-called divinity students, who were in reality draft dodgers, deserters and petty criminals, roamed the streets almost at will. Among those profiting the most were slave traders, as prices of slaves fluctuated wildly with the rise of the inflation-torn Confederate dollar. In some cases, blacks without passes were simply grabbed off the streets and sold back into slavery, even if they were legitimately free or hired out. An 1863 *Charleston Mercury* advertisement reported slaves selling for an average of nearly $1,500 per person, prices noted as "very high" even for the circumstances.

Some prognosticators have referred to wartime Richmond as "deceptively prosperous." Hotels, taverns, gambling houses and even prostitution rings were "teeming with customers," though the truth was that time was quickly running out by 1863. Families gradually lost power to profiteers, even as the desperate Confederate Congress passed laws against profiteering, in vain. The Confederate currency's rampant inflation in 1864 and 1865 was based in part on the crumbling public confidence in the slavocracy.

Near the end of the war, when retreating Confederates fired warehouses and other military stores near the river, the wind carried the embers to other buildings, and a great fire engulfed much of the central city. Up until the day before Lee's retreat, slaves had still been held at Lumpkin's awaiting auction. When black Union soldiers marched into the captured city, they stopped without orders at Lumpkin's slave jail to pay homage to the suffering that had gone on there for so many years. People nearby reportedly broke out into song: "Slavery chain done broke at last." Ironically, the grounds of Lumpkin's would become the original home of Virginia Union University after the war, a historically black university.

As for Lumpkin himself, he was desperate to preserve his human capital and save himself. He led a chained group of slaves to the depot for the Richmond and Danville Railroad, where Confederate soldiers refused to let any of them board one of the last trains. According to legend and perhaps in fact, Lumpkin's slaves were freed and were among the African Americans in Richmond who greeted the Union occupiers and, shortly thereafter, President Abraham Lincoln himself.

Not all Virginians were able to ignore the terrible trade in human flesh taking place at the very steps of their capitol. "How can an honorable mind, a patriot and a lover of his country, bear to see the ancient dominion converted into one grand menagerie, where men are to be reared for market like oxen for the shambles?" Thomas Jefferson Randolph asked. The Virginia legislature, however, often acted with complete disregard to dissenting opinion, as did the Richmond City Council.

Until the last days of the war, when Richmond was erupting in flames and Robert E. Lee was on the road to surrender at Appomattox, no one on Wall Street was listening.

CHAPTER 6

Broken Economy, Broken Human Beings

Virginia, like much of the South, was in utter economic and physical ruin at the end of the war. Many former slaves in the Richmond area, although liberated and now technically free to act as they pleased, were in reality penniless, hungry and limited in their survival options. Their vulnerability was quickly recognized by the federal government, which organized a specific agency—the Freedmen's Bureau (technically the Bureau of Refugees, Freedmen and Abandoned Lands)—to tackle the biggest problems associated with a massive human rights crisis of national importance.

Even as President Lincoln traveled through the desolate streets of Richmond along a route that took him up from Rocketts Landing, where slaves had landed for hundreds of years, and then near Wall Street, where the infamous trade had occurred, African Americans remained in a collective state of shock and disbelief. Some still had to resist the last-ditch efforts of former masters to take them away with them, in theory beyond Federal authority, still clinging to them as property. Some former slaves and free blacks wandered near the smoking ruins along the southern edge of Wall Street and must have wondered if divine retribution had come at last.

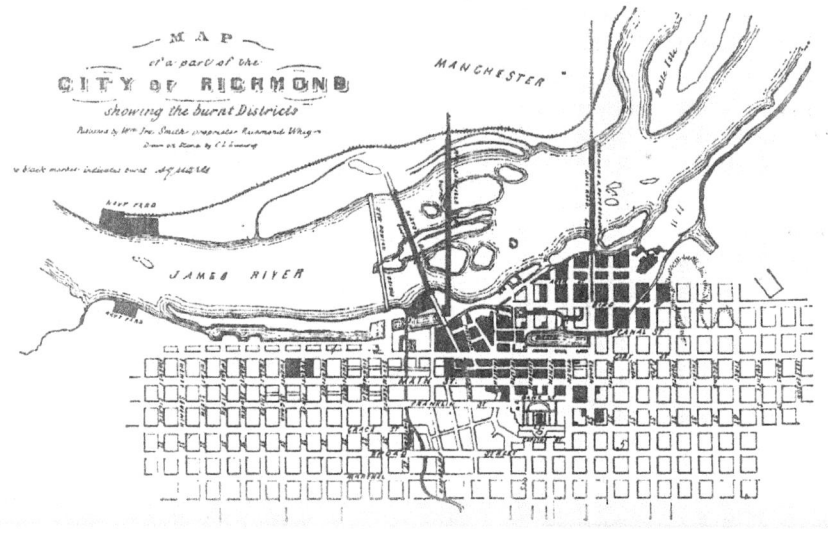

Map showing the burnt districts of Richmond in 1865. *Original by Wm. Smith of the Richmond Whig.*

Ruins of Richmond railroad depot at end of war. *From Library of Congress.*

Broken Economy, Broken Human Beings

Most whites associated with the military, the Confederate government or the slave trade had left the city. It was a revolution of sorts, but one accomplished in the ashes of a destroyed way of life.

"No event in American history matches the drama of emancipation," according to a statement by the Freedmen and Southern Society, formed in 1976 specifically to capture the essence of the revolution. "Clothed in the rhetoric of biblical prophecy and national destiny and born of a bloody civil war, it accomplished a profound social revolution." Nowhere was the revolution more evident than in post-evacuation Richmond.

The revolution did not start, however, with parades and acts of Congress. Although the Emancipation Proclamation of 1863 technically freed all "contrabands" in occupied territory (like Richmond in the spring of 1865), the reality was utter chaos. Where traders and auctioneers had bought and sold human beings, where police and provost officers had roamed the streets checking for papers, where wealthy whites had paid exorbitant prices for food in stores and restaurants while blacks went hungry, there was now only silence and quiet Federal soldiers who maintained the peace and told blacks they were now free. They did not tell them, however, what to do with that freedom or even where to eat.

Before the occupation was very old, the Freedmen's Bureau came to Richmond to organize the chaos. One of the first acts was the formation of the Freedman's Bank at 10th and Broad Streets in Richmond. In addition to providing basic services like banking, the bureau facilitated in reuniting families, formalizing marriages, securing paying labor and providing simple legal services. Federal officials had recognized quickly that granting freedom without resources to integrate blacks was a recipe for disaster. In Richmond, the Freedmen's Bureau records contain a rich story of attempts at reintegration.

Slaves were in various degrees of freedom after the surrender of Robert E. Lee at Appomattox and were in no position to fill the vacuum left by the dissolution of the Confederate government. Federal authorities in Richmond attempted to maintain order and distribute

The Richmond Slave Trade

President Lincoln arrived in Richmond shortly after evacuation to find ruins and countless freed and hungry slaves. *From Library of Congress.*

what resources were available, but most people simply had to fend for themselves. The free black community that had suffered through decades of white domination and survived a federalized Confederate slavocracy now found itself with a small natural disaster to deal with in Richmond. They opened their arms and homes and bravely tried to ease the transition for former slaves, all while survival for their own families was far from guaranteed.

The Wall Street district, although only partially destroyed by the great fire, was by and large abandoned and silent. Many of the ramshackle buildings would not survive the next decade of rebuilding; battles over Reconstruction took place in other places, and the area became even more run-down and neglected. Eventually, superhighways and parking lots would cover major portions of the district.

The shock of the end of the Civil War was so great that many people had difficulty describing it. George Lewis remembered, as a six-year-old, something of the shock as his parents, who were free blacks in Richmond, processed the incredible changes: "I shall never forget the look that came across my mother's face, but she turned around, took me in her arms, and returned to our house…There was so much noise and so much excitement."

Broken Economy, Broken Human Beings

Thomas Morris Chester, the only black newspaper reporter for a major paper during the war, wrote from the newly captured city of Richmond for the *Philadelphia Press*:

> *The day before yesterday there was a grand jubilee in the African Church...The colored people turned out in full force....Nothing can exceed the rejoicings of the negroes since the occupation of this city. They declare that they cannot realize the change; though they have long prayed for it, yet it seems impossible that it has come. Old men and women weep and shout for joy, and praise God for their deliverance through means of the Union army.*

According to a letter from Captain Brown, assistant commissioner of the Freedmen's Bureau in Richmond, there were multiple challenges that the new federal agency faced. He wrote to a military comrade who would be joining him:

> *You are hereby appointed superintendent of freedmen in the first district...You will as soon as possible take a census of all colored people within your district...Your duties will be, to protect the negroes in their rights as freeman; to see that in their present state of helplessness they are not oppressed or injured by their former masters. You will aid them by your advice in making contracts for their services...You will also let them understand that when their contracts for services are made with whites, they are under obligations to and must fulfill the same... Cultivate...among them a friendly spirit towards the citizens and their former masters...You will not issue rations to any person able to work.*

The conditions under which the Freedmen's Bureau labored were far from ideal by any measurement. Nonetheless, one cannot escape seeing the reality that former black slaves confronted—they were not yet free, by any means.

Carl Schurz, fact finder for President Johnson, wrote:

> *The efforts made to hold the negro in a state of subjection appear to have been of a particularly atrocious nature...A number of rather startling cases...proved that negroes leaving the plantations, and found on the roads, were exposed to the savagest [sic] treatment...The bewildered and terrified freedmen know what to do—to leave is death; to remain is to suffer...the cruel taskmaster, whose only interest is their labor.*

Although Schurz wrote of events in Alabama, similar occurrences were known in central Virginia and all across the conquered South.

One can argue, continuing the economic thread connected to Wall Street, that blacks traded one seriously flawed labor system for another inadequate labor system after the war, when sharecropping became common practice. In Richmond, there at least were some alternatives in the reopening factories and a supportive free black community to offer help however it could.

Individual episodes of violence—even murder—were documented in Richmond and Virginia. In 1867, General J.M. Schofield was so incensed when an examining court excused a white man for murdering a former slave that he had the individual in question arrested and brought to Richmond before a military court. "The civil courts fail," he wrote to the Freedmen's Bureau, "to give substantial justice and protection to the freedmen."

The social, economic and personal harm done to African American slaves over the course of 205 years of officially endorsed chattel bondage can't be measured, nor was it realistic to expect the terrible results to be undone immediately. The barren streets of the Wall Street district were a start at a new history, but only that. The silence of the slave markets belied the coming noise of Reconstruction and other battles that would be fought well into the twentieth century.

CHAPTER 7

Legacy of Wall Street

Perhaps it was and is fortuitous that the area around Wall Street was partially burned to the ground at the end of the war and the rest of it razed within a few years. Very few physical traces remain today, and the scars of a terrible past are now buried in ground surrounded by tall buildings and interstate highways. Some might argue convincingly, however, that it instead contributed to a collective amnesia that, along with the southern cult of the "Lost Cause," created far more problems after the war than it resolved; that in fact, it made it possible to ignore and forget the past.

The legacy of Wall Street cannot be found in the ground as much as it can be found in the events that the traditions of a southern slave economy bequeathed to a Reconstruction Richmond. This tradition included passive resistance, continued racism and manipulation of the free labor market (including sharecropping practices that resulted in something similar to antebellum slavery).

There are groups in Richmond that have fought tenaciously to preserve and maintain the history of blacks and the slave trade, such as the Defenders for Freedom, Justice and Equality (DFJE), and their efforts have helped save the "Burial Ground for Negroes" in the north of the Wall Street area. But these efforts also seem to face an inexplicable inertia, a ghostly resistance that seemingly stems from nowhere but that ultimately has to be lodged in part within entrenched ideas inside of real human beings who make real decisions or decide on inaction as the course of least resistance.

The legacy of Wall Street is a difficult history to commemorate, as it involves memories that are painful, controversial and unsettling. A stated goal of the Civil War Sesquicentennial Commission is "to promote historic tourism to Richmond," yet like the unopened National Museum of Slavery, the commission faces the contradiction that has long been associated with the Civil War: people are interested in battles, campaigns and military heroics; they are not as interested in what those campaigns were fought over. ("Visitors want battles; not social history" one headline declared.)

Scenes from the aftermath of war. The Freedmen's Union Industrial School, Richmond. *From Library of Congress.*

Legacy of Wall Street

Ruins of the city after the war, just west of where the modern slave history trail crosses. *From Library of Congress.*

In 2011, seventeen interpretive signs were erected along the slave trail from Manchester and in the Wall Street district, correcting what some labeled a "historical slight." According to reporter Steve Szkotak, this event was symbolic for many reasons, "casting light on Richmond's often-overlooked role in the commerce of slavery." He also noted how "unpleasant" this chapter of local history remains, in spite of the fact that many reasonable people agree that it is a story that needs to be told.

"Slavery was the economic engine of the South and the epicenter of slavery was right here," Szkotak quotes Virginia General Assembly

The Richmond Slave Trade

Richmond burning at the close of the war; Wall Street district is just to the right. *From Library of Congress.*

delegate Delores L. McQuinn as saying at the dedication, standing beside a bronze sculpture known as the *Reconciliation Statue*, which remembers the triangle points in the transatlantic slave trade (Benin; Liverpool, England; and Richmond). One of the triangle points, of course, was Wall Street in Richmond. Of Wall Street, McQuinn says, "There's a presence there, a spirit."

The pain of Wall Street continues post-abolition and post–Civil War. Former Richmond mayor Tim Kaine perhaps said it most bluntly: "Our particular legacy causes us some real problems… In a lot of ways, the Civil War has been an albatross around our necks." Kaine is one of the few in positions of power who seems to be brutally honest. "A lot of people don't want to acknowledge the centrality of slavery to the Confederate cause…Everyone knows that slavery was evil, but nobody wants to think that their ancestors weren't noble people."

Legacy of Wall Street

In 1993, the Emancipation Proclamation went on public display in Washington, D.C., at the National Archives building—for the first time since 1863. Although the reason for not displaying it was due to preservation concerns, it is also emblematic of a nation that can't fully heal from the wounds that were opened and excised in 1865 through fire and military defeat. *Time* magazine in 2011 said it this way: "North and South shared the burden of slavery, and after the war, they shared in forgetting about it."

Many individuals interviewed during the course of research on Wall Street expressed relief that the district had burned to the ground in 1865: "I think it's better for everyone involved," one city resident declared. The ghosts of Wall Street remain anyway.

Today's citizens of Richmond continue to find ways to remember the past—candlelight vigils, additional archaeological digs, recovering the sacred ground of the African Burial Ground—but the larger work of permanent healing remains.

CONCLUSION
The Opening of the National Slavery Museum

The opening of a National Slavery Museum in Fredericksburg, Virginia, remains problematic as of the publication of this book. One wonders, after hearing the story of Wall Street, if similar forces to those present immediately after the war remain in play, even 147 years after the fact. There are practical issues, to be sure, including management decisions, funding challenges and sponsorship. Yet other museums have opened, in spite of such challenges, and the National Slavery Museum remains just a possibility at this time, a wish unfulfilled.

Former Virginia governor L. Douglas Wilder, who had the inspiration for the idea in 1992, believes the project will come to fruition:

> *We intend to build the Unites States National Slavery Museum. And we will build it on the beautiful piece of land we own off the Rappahannock River in Fredericksburg… This museum is too important to Virginia and this country for any of us currently involved with its creation to even consider surrendering to the current economic conditions*

Conclusion

that have made finishing this project a more complex task than we could have originally foreseen...Many people who share our vision have donated priceless artifacts...They must be properly displayed as a looking glass into a time that must not be forgotten or repeated.

With the physical possibility of recovering Wall Street not a feasible alternative, and the limitations of the slave trail (some artifacts along the trail have already been stolen), the possibility of a National Slavery Museum would seem to be a logical way to preserve the past and to reconstruct what still remains an incomplete and misunderstood history. There could be little doubt that the museum would have numerous artifacts and displays relating directly and indirectly to the slave trade in the Wall Street district of Richmond.

Although the silence of 1865 along Wall Street continues in many ways in 2011 (except for the efforts of those like the DFJE), one might pause and ask the question: have Americans fully come to grips with what happened there? Perhaps a National Slavery Museum will provide part of the answer.

References

Berwanger, Eugene H. *As They Saw Slavery*. Malibar, FL: Robert E. Krieger Publishing Co., 1973.
Britton, Rick. "Edward Coles and the 'Peculiar Institution.'" *Albemarle Magazine*, February–March 1998, 60–66.
Cabell, Robert H. "Slave Health Certificate" [manuscript]. Charlottesville: University of Virginia Library Special Collections, 1837.
Civil War Richmond. www.mdgorman.com.
Civil War Traveler. www.civilwartraveler.com.
Conrad, A.H., and J.R. Meyer. *The Economics of Slavery and Other Studies in Econometric History*. Chicago: Aldine Publishing Company, 1964.
Crowe, Eyre. *With Thackeray in America*. London: Cassell and Company, 1893.
Dabney, Virginius. *Richmond, the Story of a City*. New York: Doubleday & Company, 1976.
Defenders for Freedom, Justice and Equality. *An Appeal to All People of Good Will: The Case for Reclaiming Richmond's Shockoe Bottom*. Richmond, VA: DFJE, 2008.
Digital Scholarship Lab. "Hidden Patterns of the Civil War." dsl.richmond.edu/civilwar/slavemarket.html.

References

Duke, Maurice, and Daniel P. Jordan, eds. *A Richmond Reader: 1733–1983*. Chapel Hill: University of North Carolina Press, 1983.

Edwards, Ana. "Wall Street of Confederacy." Personal communication, September 22, 2011.

Fogel, Robert William, and Stanley L. Engerman. *Time on the Cross: The Economics of American Negro Slavery*. New York: W.W. Norton & Co., 1989.

Foundation for Teaching Economics. "The Economics of Slavery." www.fte.org.

Franklin, J.H., and L. Schweninger. *Runaway Slaves: Rebels on the Plantation, 1790–1860*. Oxford, UK: Oxford University Press, 1999.

Free Lance-Star [Fredericksburg, VA], various articles, 2008–11.

A Guide to the Bell Tavern Records. ead.lib.virginia.edu/vivaxtf/view?docId=lva/vi00474.xml;query=;brand=default.

Historical Marker Database. www.hmdb.org.

The Historical Shop (various manuscripts). Metairie, LA. www.historicalshop.com.

Huger, Frank. *The Civil War Letters of a Confederate Artillery Officer*. Edited by Thomas K. Tate. Jefferson, NC: McFarland, 2011.

Jefferson, Thomas. *Notes on the State of Virginia*. N.p., 1781.

Johnson, C., P. Smith, et. al. *Africans in America: America's Journey through Slavery*. New York: Harcourt Brace and Co., 2006.

Johnson, Linwood. "Early History: Slavery" [unpublished manuscript]. Richmond, VA, 2009.

Koman, Rita G. *The Freedmen's Bureau: Catalyst for Freedom?* Los Angeles: University of California, National Center for History in the Schools, 2002.

Lankford, Nelson. *Richmond Burning: The Last Days of the Confederate Capital*. New York: Viking, 2002.

Levine, Bruce. *Confederate Emancipation: Southern Plans to Free and Arm Slaves During the Civil War.* Oxford, UK: Oxford University Press, 2006.

Lewis, B. "Symbols Dividing a City: Honoring Southern Legacy, Richmond Courts Controversy." *Austin American-Statesmen*, 1999.

REFERENCES

Little, John P. *Richmond: The Capitol of Virginia: Its History*. Richmond, VA: MacFarlene & Ferguson, 1851.
Malvasi, Mark. "My Brother's Keeper: Proslavery Thought and the Southern Critique of Modernity" [manuscript]. Randolph-Macon College, 2006.
Manarin, Louis H. *Richmond at War: The Minutes of the City Council 1861–1865*. Chapel Hill: University of North Carolina Press, 1966.
Minchinton, Walter, and Celia King, eds. *Virginia Slave-Trade Statistics: 1698–1775*. Richmond: Virginia State Library, 1984.
Mjagkij, Nina, ed. *Organizing Black America: An Encyclopedia of African American Associations*. New York: Routledge, 2001.
Museum of the Confederacy. Various documents [manuscript]. Richmond, VA. "Accounting sheet for period of December..." 1857.
———. "American Life Insurance and Trust Company policy held..." 1858.
———. "Bill of Expenses from Mr. C. Coleman..." 1852.
———. "Bill of Sale from Alexander Payne to Robert Garnett..." (1847)
———. "Correspondence Deas-Archer Family..." 1842.
———. "Correspondence Tompkins Family..." 1848.
———. "Handbill Advertising Slave Insurance..." circa 1850s.
———. "Hiring Certificate for Slaves Gabriel..." 1855.
———. "Letter from A. Dudley..." 1860.
———. "Letter from Charles Woolfolk of Caroline County..." 1853.
———. "Letter from Col. T.J. Gregory..." 1853.
———. "Letter from James Yates of North Carolina..." 1854.
———. "Letter from W.H. Mosby..." 1853.
———. "Mss, Receipt of Transfer of Slaves..." 1857.
———. "Receipt for Negro Hire..." 1853.
———. "Receipt for $1,290 Received of J.D. Fendrent Brothers..." 1859.
———. "Receipt for Purchase of Arthur..." 1836.
———. "Sale of Slave Soloman, Sept. 1842..." 1842.

References

———. "Slave Sale Receipt William Powers…" 1857.
———. "Statement under Oath by Henry F. Clabaugh…" 1854.
———. "State of North Carolina Court of Pleas…" 1860.
———. "Terms of Leasing and Renting…" 1853.
National Park Service. "Richmond Speaks: Voices from the Home Front." *Richmond Civil War Visitor*, 2006.
National Register of Historic Places Multiple Property Documentation Form. NPS Form 10-900-b. "The Slave Trade as a Commercial Enterprise in Richmond, Virginia, MPS #127-6196."
Oates, Stephen B. *The Fires of Jubilee: Nat Turner's Fierce Rebellion*. New York: New American Library, 1975.
Olmsted, Frederick Law. *A Journey in the Seaboard Slave States; With Remarks on Their Economy*. New York: Dix & Edwards, 1856.
Richardson, Selden. *Built by Blacks: African American Architecture and Neighborhoods in Richmond*. Charleston, SC: The History Press, 2008.
RichmondGov.com.
Richmond Times-Dispatch, various articles, 2008–11.
Scanlon, James. "Slavery at R-MC." Personal communication, February 21, 2011.
Schwarz, Philip J. "Timeline of the Slave Trade in Richmond and Virginia." www.library.vcu.edu/jbc/speccoll/slavery/timeline.html.
Snell, Mark A. "Toward Statehood: Western Virginia on the Eve of the War." *Hallowed Ground* 12, no. 3 (2011): 24–33.
Stamp, K.M., ed. "Records of Ante-bellum Southern Plantations from the Revolution through the Civil War." Microfiche. Raleigh, NC: Duke University, 2000.
Szkotak, Steve. "Markers Tell of Richmond's Slave-Trading Past." HamptonRoads.com.
Takagi, Midora. *Rearing Wolves to Our Own Destruction: Slavery in Richmond, Virginia, 1782–1865*. Charlottesville: University of Virginia Press, 2002.
Templeton & Goodwin. "Account Book of Slave Traders in Richmond, VA" [manuscript]. Charlottesville: University of Virginia Library Special Collections, 1851.
The Terrible Transformation. PBS.

References

Trammell, Jack. "Inns and Outs of Civil War Richmond." *America's Civil War* (September 1996).

———. "Wall Street of the Confederacy." *Washington-Times*, February 12, 2005, D4.

Turpin & Yarbrough. "List of Slaves Bought between the Years 1851 and 1860" [manuscript]. Charlottesville: University of Virginia Library Special Collections, 1860.

The Virginia Defender, various issues, 2011.

Von Drehle, David. "The Civil War 1861–2011: The Way We Weren't." *Time*, April 18, 2011, 40–51.

Ward, Harry M. *Richmond: An Illustrated History*. Northridge, CA: Windsor Publications, 1985.

White, Ralph R. *Seeing the Scars of Slavery in the Natural Environment: An Interpretive Guide to the Manchester Slave Trail along the James River in Richmond*. Richmond, VA: Richmond Parks and Recreation Department, 2002.

Workers of the Writers' Program of the Work Projects Administration in the State of Virginia. *Virginia: A Guide to the Old Dominion*. Richmond: Virginia State Library and Archives in cooperation with the Virginia Center for the Book, published by authority of the Library Board, 1992.

About the Author

Jack Trammell was born in Berea, Kentucky, and is descended from generations of Appalachian farmers who migrated from Normandy through England and Virginia. He is a professor, researcher and writer, as well as a small family farmer currently residing in central Virginia with his wife and seven children (Daniel, Alec, Bethany, Maddie, Mary, Chris and Hannah, and of course, Audrie!).

He has more than twenty-one books to his credit, ranging from textbooks for students in gifted programs (math and history) to award-winning Appalachian writing (Jesse Stuart poetry award, etc.). His published credits include research articles in education and sociology journals (related to disability studies), as well as hundreds of articles, short stories and poems. For almost seven years, he wrote a regular military history column for the *Washington Times*.

His education includes a BA in political science at Grove City College, a master's degree in history education at Virginia Commonwealth University, a special education certificate from the University of Virginia and a PhD again from VCU. Most recently, he was a visiting scholar at the DuPont-funded Summer Seminar at the National Center for the Humanities.

His current projects include a vampire novel, selling three manuscripts that are book-ready and finishing several research projects. Recently, he has been traveling to Eastern Europe as a disability accommodation consultant.

He can be reached at jacktrammell@yahoo.com.

www.ingramcontent.com/pod-product-compliance
Lightning Source LLC
Chambersburg PA
CBHW060812100426
42813CB00004B/1044